REIKI AT HAND

Teresa Collins

THE COLLINS

Published by The Collins Press, Carey's Lane, The Huguenot
Quarter, Cork, 1998

Printed in Ireland by Sci Print, Shannon

Jacket design by Upper Case Ltd., Cornmarket Street, Cork

ISBN: 1-898256-40-3

To my mother, Eileen,
in deep appreciation for the gift of faith

Acknowledgements

To all my Reiki friends who shared their experiences with me, and made this book possible.

Graphics are by Tim O'Donovan, Conceptual Design and the cover illustration, entitled *Receiving Gentle Medicine*, is by Charles Frizzell. Edited by Claire O'Mahony, Writing and Editing and Áine Collins.

CONTENTS

any or all levels of Reiki, he/she acts as a channel of universal energy, increasing the life force on the whole planet. This results in increasing the individual's own life force and releasing negative forms of existence such as worry, fear, anger, shame or self doubt, as well as increasing physical health. In this way universal wellbeing is enhanced. For this reason, I honour all practitioners of Reiki, both those who are actively practising and those who have taken the workshops.

TERESA COLLINS
FEBRUARY 1998

LEVEL I

CHAPTER 1

The History of Reiki

Reiki comes from two Japanese words, *Rei* which means Universal Life Energy, and *Ki* which means a key or an opening. Reiki can then be interpreted as a key to universal energy.

The literal definition is the channelling of natural life energy through a human being to another living being or object, or the channelling of love in the form of natural energy.

Reiki can be traced back to Buddha, who lived in northern India approximately 600 BCE, although Reiki may have existed in earlier times. Buddha was a great spiritual teacher who healed the sick and raised people from the dead. He spent his adult life exploring the nature of suffering, and teaching ways to minimise its effect. His teachings are held sacred. Although Reiki can be traced back to Buddha, and was practised widely in Tibet about 2,500 years ago, it may have existed prior to his time. For some unknown reason, Reiki was not practised, to our knowledge, for many years until it was rediscovered by Dr Mikao Usui in Japan.

DR MIKAO USUI
Dr Usui was born in 1865. As an adult he travelled to several Western countries and to China to study. At one

time he went to Mount Kuri-Yama for a 21 day retreat to fast and meditate. At the end of this period he suddenly felt the great Reiki energy at the top of his head, which led to the Reiki Healing System. He first used Reiki on himself and then tried it on his family. Since it worked well for various ailments, he decided to share his knowledge with the public at large. He opened a clinic in Tokyo in 1922. He treated countless patients and hosted workshops to spread his knowledge. In September 1923 a devastating earthquake shook Tokyo. Soon, his clinic became too small to handle the throng of patients and he built a new one outside Tokyo in Nakano.

He received invitations to distant towns and villages, as his fame spread. During his stay in Fukuyama he was hit by a fatal stroke in 1926. He was 61 years old.

Dr Usui felt that as well as practising Reiki, one should also follow these five principles:

– *Just for today do not worry*
– *Just for today do not anger*
– *Just for today honour your teachers, your parents and your elders*
– *Just for today earn your living honestly*
– *Just for today show an attitude of gratitude*

JUST FOR TODAY DO NOT WORRY

Doctors say that most illnesses are stress induced. Stress originates in the mind and it is a product of our thought processes. Normally we spend our mental energy trying to manipulate our lives in order to achieve specific results. However, very often factors are involved which we cannot control. Dr Usui very wisely asks us to work hard and leave the rest to God or to the 'universal energy'. All our needs will be met, though perhaps not exactly as we had planned. Some of these thoughts are

11

expressed in the prayer – *God give me the strength to accept the things I cannot change, the courage to change the things I can, and the wisdom to know the difference.*

The hardest part about this prayer is the complete surrender of control that is required as it feels like the surrender of personal will. However, when one is channelling the 'universal energy', it is very difficult to channel this energy without experiencing the flow of energy in one's own life. It is best to inform the energy of what one needs in one's life, and then to surrender to that process. A saying in new-age thinking urges us to *let the universe take care of the details.* The reasoning behind this saying is that the universe has a much bigger picture of life than the individual. When one learns *not to worry,* there is so much more energy to use in a positive fashion. Worry never accomplishes anything positive, but creates weaknesses in our world.

JUST FOR TODAY DO NOT ANGER

Many people store suppressed unconscious emotions in their bodies. Life is structured to release these feelings, so that people can come home to who they really are – *channels of love.* When people or situations come into one's life and once suppressed emotions are felt, for example anger, sadness, grief or abandonment, often the person or the situation is thought to be responsible for triggering these emotions. However, life is a mirror that reflects back one's own unconsciousness. So, instead of reacting to that person or situation with blame, one should give thanks for discovering a hidden aspect of oneself, and, if possible, to let go of it with love. When one feels anger, note it and release it with love, avoid projecting it onto the person or situation that triggered it. Sometimes it is necessary to physically move it out of the body through manual labour or physical exercise.

Other people find it helpful to explore the roots of their emotions either through discussion with friends, or through reading or professional counselling. However, the important thing is never to project the emotion onto another person or situation. It is only through each individual's willingness to live in harmony on the earth that universal harmony will be achieved.

JUST FOR TODAY HONOUR YOUR PARENTS, TEACHERS AND ELDERS

This principle encourages us to honour all people, all creatures and all situations in life, as everything in life teaches us. Unfortunately certain people experience abuse by their teachers or even by their parents. This principle does not ask them to respect the treatment they received, but instead to try and grow from that experience, to forgive the perpetrator, and to give themselves great compassion.

In Japan in the 1800s the elderly were respected but in our culture today we are much less likely to practise this principle, as there is more of a tendency to honour youth.

JUST FOR TODAY LIVE HONESTLY

Life is lived through us. We are all channels of life. Unless there is an equal balance of giving and receiving in our lives, a certain amount of stagnation occurs in our energy. In order to remain healthy we must balance both giving and receiving, and in this way we can live our lives honestly.

SHOW GRATITUDE TO EVERY LIVING THING

Some of the richest people in the world are the least happy, whereas some of the poorest people in the world are the most peaceful. This is because when one has the

13

least amount, one appreciates it more, as one is really aware of it. When one lives in excess, greed is promoted. Unless we say thankyou for all our blessings in life such as our health, our material possessions and the beauty of nature, we do not really feel as if these are a gift to us, despite the fact that nothing in life stays constant. However, when we thank the source for everything in our lives, we recognise that we are blest and we feel appreciative and loved.

These principles are the means by which all Reiki practitioners and teachers stay healthy.

Dr Usui founded a Reiki organisation called the Usui Reiki Healing Method Society or in Japanese, *Usui Reiki Ryoho Gakkai*, or *Usui Shiki Reiki Ryoho*, and acted as its first president. That organisation continues to the present day and its president is Ms Kimiko Koyama.

One of Dr Usui's disciples was a retired naval officer called Dr Chujiro Hayashi, who was responsible for releasing knowledge of the Reiki to the West.

DR CHUJIRO HAYASHI

Dr Hayashi received his Reiki Masters degree in 1925 at the age of 47. He opened a clinic in Tokyo, and had several practitioners working with him and also working in the neighbourhood.

In 1934 a woman called Ms Hawayo Takata was successfully treated in his clinic. As she came from Hawaii she had difficulty accessing his clinic, so she asked to be taught Reiki to enable her to maintain her health whilst at home. In 1936, she trained in Level I Reiki. The following year she trained in Level II Reiki and in 1938 she became a Reiki Master. Dr Hayashi trained 5–18 teachers during his time as a Reiki Master. He had already prophesied the outbreak of World War II and he felt that a Reiki Master needed to live outside of Japan. He died in 1941 and Ms Takata took charge of Reiki in the West until her death in 1980. Ms Takata taught Reiki in the United States, Canada and in Europe. She initiated 22 Reiki Masters, including her granddaughter, Phyllis Furomoto.

There are now Reiki practitioners and teachers in almost every country of the world. Anyone can learn Reiki and everyone has the ability to perform it. The Reiki classes simply bring out that which is already inherent in a person. It simply turns on a light, since the lighting fixtures, as it were, are already in place.

CHAPTER 2

How Reiki Works and What it Achieves

Hawayo Takato described Reiki as a radionic wave that comes from *The Great Spirit*. Everything that exists is composed of energy. The physical component of an atom is only about 1% – the other 99% is composed of energy. There is a rule in physics that says: Energy must always balance. This means that when high energy and low energy are connected up, by means of a conductor, the energy flows from high to low until both equalise.

Following Reiki training, a Reiki practitioner becomes a conductor of energy. When someone or something is touched by a Reiki practitioner, energy is drawn into that person or object if it is low in energy. This energy has a healing effect. However, the person or object must be willing, on a soul level, to receive this energy, otherwise the energy will not be drawn in.

Reiki will heal almost any condition as long as the person is willing to receive the energy. It is known to be successful in the treatment of strains, sprains, torn cartilages, fractures, chest conditions, joint conditions, misalignments of the spine, bowel problems, problems with sexual organs and with the menses, skin problems, stress, mild depression and for people who have had strokes, amongst other conditions. It does not have a

100% success rate, and it is not an instant cure. In most cases, however, there is a considerable relief of discomfort and the clients have a significant improvement in the quality of their lives. The longer a problem has been present in the body, usually the longer it takes to heal. For illnesses that are present for more than three months, the client is often asked to train in Reiki I, as if daily treatment is necessary, it is easier and more cost efficient if the client can perform it on him/her self.

This brings us to question why Reiki does not work all the time? Healing is a very complex issue. Sometimes one technique/therapy will not benefit a client, whereas another technique or therapy will. In other cases, on a subconscious level, a person may choose illness over health, as there may be something to learn from the experience of illness that the person needs. In Reiki, we never judge ourselves or the client if we not do achieve the desired results. We simply give five Reiki sessions and if the client does not feel any improvement, we do not proceed any further.

It is important to stress that Reiki does not only heal disease or illness – it also makes an already good situation better. It can be used to maintain personal health, improve a business or improve personal relationships. Reiki, then, is a tool of empowerment that can be used both personally and professionally.

CHAPTER 3

Levels of Reiki

There are three levels of Reiki. These are simply Level I, Level II and Level III which is sometimes called the *'Master's Level'*.

LEVEL I

This course opens the Reiki channels in the practitioner to allow for the channelling of Reiki. Of all three courses, it is probably the one people remember the most, as it is the first time that they experience themselves as channels of Reiki. This is a very empowering process.

This course is normally run over two days. The core of Level I is four attunements. *Attunements* attune the body to become a channel of Reiki, almost in the same way as a radio is tuned. Nothing is physically removed or added. The body is simply structured to pick up a different frequency of energy. The remainder of the workshop consists of discussion, practise and some teachers use visualisation techniques. The attunements, however, are the only essential part of the workshop. They are very simple and each one lasts about three minutes. They are performed whilst sitting and the practitioner remains fully clothed and conscious the whole time.

Level I initially opens the Reiki channels. This happens during the workshop and for the following 21 days. During this time the practitioner may notice his/her body go through a healing experience of some kind. When this takes place physically the practitioner may develop a chest cold, a sore throat or a slight skin irritation. When it occurs on the emotional level, the practitioner may notice him/her self experiencing stronger negative and positive emotions than usual. Once the 21 days are up the body adjusts to its new status.

The practitioner is now able to channel Reiki to other people, animals, plants or objects, but cannot charge a fee. It is necessary to take Level II to do so. Level II can be taken 21 days after Level I, but it is best to wait about six weeks. Level II teaches three Reiki symbols. The first symbol, known as the *Empowerment* symbol, can be used to turn the energy on and to increase its intensity. The second symbol, the *Mental/Emotional Healing* symbol, is used to alter the frequency of energy, so that it has a calming effect on the client. It is also used to release addictions. The third symbol is known as the *Long-distance* symbol and it is used to collapse time and distance. *This means that a practitioner will be just as effective 10,000 miles away from a client, as they would be in the same room!*

This course is usually taught over two days or four half days. It takes three months to integrate Level II Reiki. The practitioner channels the energy much more strongly, and is now allowed to charge a fee.

The final level, Level III or the *Master's Workshop* can be taken one year after Level II. Here the practitioner is given a fourth Reiki symbol and this has two uses. Once again it amplifies the energy further but it is also used to initiate people into Reiki. Nobody can practise Reiki without first being initiated by a Reiki Master.

19

CHAPTER 4

Questions Commonly Asked About Level I Reiki

Q. Why should I take a course in Reiki?
A. Once a person has been initiated into Reiki, Reiki energy will flow through that person always. This energy has an energising effect, so that even if one never practises Reiki on another person, one will have greater impact in one's own personal and professional life.

Using Reiki as a healing device on oneself for just 20 minutes every day assists in relaxation and in maintaining one's health. Should a practitioner go on to take Level II, Reiki gives him/her a healing tool, not only for one's own body but for every aspect of one's life, past, present and future. It gives one a sense of empowerment.

Q. What teacher should I study with?
A. Reiki is the same coming from all teachers. When choosing a teacher, the practitioner should choose one with whom he or she feels comfortable. Reiki is an ongoing education, so the teacher should have regular support evenings. It is best to study with a teacher who will be available for at least a year afterwards for consultation purposes.

Q. Is there any danger from taking a Reiki course?
A. During the Reiki I course, channels will become available in the practitioner's body for channelling Reiki. This takes a certain amount of energy from the body to adapt to this new ability. The process continues for 21 days after taking the course. Some people find that they are more tired than usual during this time or emotionally more vulnerable. It is best, therefore, to avoid taking the course when one is either emotionally or physically stressed.

Q. Will this course affect my spiritual beliefs in any way and is there a spiritual dogma attached to it?
A. There is no spiritual dogma attached to Reiki. One of the Reiki principles is to honour our ancestors, so in the history of Reiki we always give credit to Buddha for having brought Reiki into existence and for passing it down to us through Dr Usui. Reiki makes one much more aware of the non-physical component of life and its impact, and in that way it strengthens one's spirituality, however one expresses it.

Q. Should I have a medical background?
A. Anyone can practise Reiki and a medical background is not necessary. You should, however, be aware of what you are working with, on an anatomical level. For Level I Reiki, consulting an anatomy reference book will suffice. For Level II practitioners, it is advisable to take an anatomy course.

Q. Will I feel the Reiki energy?
A. Most people feel the energy flowing through them during the Level I course. It is felt as a change of temperature in the hands and as a tingling in certain parts of the body. The practitioner also notices various

21

sensations in the body as he/she channels the Reiki energy. Occasionally, a practitioner cannot feel the energy in him/her self, but the person receiving the energy will feel it. It is usual to feel it within three months of taking the Level I course.

Finally, it is helpful to receive at least one Reiki session from your intended Reiki teacher before taking Level I Reiki. This enables you to be more aware of what Reiki is and become familiar with the teacher.

CHAPTER 5

Level I for Practitioners

The core of the Level I workshop is the four attunements. The experience of becoming attuned is unique to each practitioner and each attunement can be a different experience too.

The most common experience of an attunement is one of peace and deep relaxation. Some practitioners will have visual experiences varying from seeing colours, green fields or scenes from their lives. A practitioner's eyes are closed during an attunement and these scenes are seen with the *third eye* or the *mind's eye*.

Sometimes an attunement can affect the emotional body, with the practitioner releasing blocked emotions from the past. These emotions can vary from boredom, anger, sadness, joy and hope to ecstasy.

There is of course a physical response in the body. This can be as simple as feeling hot or cold, or as complex as a re-emergence of old aches and pains. The most common site of discomfort is the throat and the discomfort can last for up to 21 days after the workshop.

Some students will feel light-headed and on the verge of fainting. Should this happen, it is a good idea to open your eyes, breathe deeply and call the teacher.

Occasionally the energy will create a physical movement in the body and this is always safe, and it is best to surrender to it. Some practitioners will feel nothing at all during an attunement and this is also normal, as not every attunement gives rise to sensory feedback. Some attunements take place silently and these attunements are equally effective. No matter what one feels, it is appropriate for that moment. The attunements are given over a two-day period, one each morning and another each afternoon. The practitioner's body controls the attunements and, therefore, they are always safe.

MOST OFTEN ASKED QUESTIONS DURING LEVEL I REIKI

Q. How do the Attunements work?
A. Attunements are similar to jump starting a car when the battery has gone dead.

A strong charge of energy is sent into the practitioner through the teacher and it activates an ability that is already there. The energy has to pass through four doorways in the practitioner. The first doorway is in the heart and it is opened in the first attunement. The second doorway is in the throat and the second attunement opens it. This attunement is often accompanied by a sore throat, which can last up to 21 days. The third attunement opens a door at the back of the eyes and it is often accompanied by a light show of some kind. The fourth and final attunement opens a door at the top of the head where Reiki enters the practitioner's head. The practitioner often notices a swirling haze above the crown of the head as this door opens.

Q. How does Reiki work?
A. Reiki works on the physics principle that energy always seeks to balance itself. The client's body may be considered as negative energy and the air around it as positive energy. The practitioner acts as a channel or

conductor and energy is drawn into the client, provided that the client, on a soul level, is willing to receive it. This energy is a positive benign energy and as one works with Reiki, one feels a very loving quality inherent in it. Hawayo Takato taught that Reiki was the energy of God.

Q. Does Reiki always work?

A. Reiki works as long as the person is willing to draw it in, and if, on a soul level, it is time for healing to take place. However, Reiki works on four planes of existence: the physical; mental; emotional, and spiritual. It may sometimes take an apparently convoluted route in healing, and this is something that the practitioner cannot control. For example, if a client were treated for whiplash, he/she may feel, after four sessions, that his/her pain has not diminished but that he/she is sleeping better, has more energy and feels that he/she can cope with life more easily. Typically, after four more sessions the pain improves and the neck movement increases. In this case it seems that in order to release the physical blockage, the shock needs to be released first from the emotional body. If methods other than Reiki are used, a client quite often has the physical ability to move his/her neck, for example, but is reluctant to do so. This is possibly because the shock has not been removed from the body. Conversely Reiki may work on the physical level from the start, but on an area of the body other than that where the symptoms are located. Quite often when clients come with knee problems, the energy will work on the lower back. This is because the cause of the knee problem emanates from the back, and the effect is experienced in the knee. Reiki will always go to the cause of the problem. When treating clients with Reiki you should notice some response to the treatment after four or five sessions. The first three treatments may make the symptoms more pronounced, but this is quite normal with any treatment technique as treatment increases blood flow to the damaged area. However, after four or five treatments the client should notice some improvement. Once improvement is experienced it is an indication to carry on with further treatments. If the client is not happy with the results, discontinue after five sessions. If the condition has existed in the body for longer than three months, it may be necessary to give six treatments before the client can experience any improvement in his/her condition. When in doubt, continue treatment for up to six sessions before discontinuing it.

Q. How do I know when I am channelling Reiki?
A. Reiki is almost always accompanied by some sensory change in the body, which would not arise if one was not channelling energy. Initially the most common sensation experienced with Level I Reiki is tingling in the hands and fingers, or soreness around the neck or shoulders. This is caused by the channels opening and more energy coming to these parts of the body. You may also notice energy in other areas of the body.

You may also pick up other people's aches and pains for a few seconds. In the beginning it is difficult to differentiate between which sensations belong to the practitioner, and which sensations belong to the client. However, once the practitioner has given three or four Reiki treatments he/she will be able to identify how the energy affects him/her and those sensations that are not normal or familiar to the practitioner are symptoms that he/she is picking up from the client.

When a pracitioner firsts starts channelling Reiki, for example, the energy could concentrate in the stomach area. This could last for two to three months. For roughly the next two months it could concentrate in the head. Therefore, if energy goes to other areas of your body, you can be confident that this is information being received from the client.

Q. Why do my hands get very hot when I am channelling Reiki?
A. Energy moving through the arms and hands creates a physiological change resulting in a change in temperature. Sometimes the hands get hot, sometimes very cold. Sometimes the hands can seem very hot to the practitioner but icy cold to the client. This happens mainly when treating the back of the head. It has been my experience that Reiki can often appear cold when the client's energy is very low and often warms up as his/her energy improves after a few Reiki sessions.

Q. Why do I feel so relaxed when channelling Reiki?
A. The most common effect of Reiki is to induce relaxation and sleep. This is felt not only by the client but also by the practitioner as the energy is drawn into the client through the practitioner. A certain amount of the Reiki energy will remain in the practitioner and will have a relaxing and healing effect on the practitioner. Often the only difference between giving and receiving a Reiki session is that the client receiving the Reiki energy can go off to sleep while the practitioner, for the most part, must remain alert. It is a mutually healing and relaxing experience for both the practitioner and the client, as both receive the Reiki energy.

Q. Why is a Reiki session given mainly in silence?
A. Some relevant conversation may take place during a Reiki session. It is best not to chat socially as the deeper the client surrenders to the Reiki, the more valuable the

session will be. Reiki releases energy stored in the tissues. Any unnecessary conversation inhibits this process of release. Sometimes the release of energy creates pain or discomfort and the client should feel free to discuss this with the practitioner.

Q. What do I need to do before treating a client?
A. Before giving a Reiki treatment, the practitioner should prepare him/her self and the treatment room. The treatment room should be clean and reasonably warm. It creates a healing atmosphere if there is a bunch of flowers or a lighted candle in the room. In Level II you learn a blessing for the room using one of the symbols. With Level I Reiki, a sacred space can be created in the treatment room using whatever manner is traditional for the practitioner. Some may use a sacred object, some use water, some say a prayer or do a visualisation in the room before giving a treatment. This process sets an atmosphere of rest and healing which the client will experience when he/she enters. The practitioner should prepare him/her self by sitting quietly for a few minutes before the client arrives. I teach my practitioners to *centre and ground* themselves before giving a treatment.

Centring is a simple process of breathing in through the nose and out through a relaxed mouth, while concentrating the mind on the rising and falling of the abdomen with each breath. This relaxes and focuses the mind of the practitioner.

Grounding is simply imagining energy flowing out through the feet and tail-bone, and going deep into the earth. This opens the grounding cords of the body so any excess or unwanted energy can be quickly released. This visualisation is done before treating a client or done once or twice during the Reiki session. It is not unusual during the Reiki session to feel tingling in your feet and tailbone. This is the energy exiting through the grounding cords.

Q. Can a practitioner take on the client's symptoms

A. During a Reiki session a practitioner can become one with the spiritual, physical, emotional and/or mental state of the client for brief moments. It is very important to become aware of one's own state on all these levels so that the practitioner can differentiate between his/her own processing and that of the client. It is a great help to experience the client's symptoms both from an academic and a humanitarian point of view. The practitioner should thank the energy for bringing this information and, if it does not leave quickly, ground it through their grounding cords. If the symptoms persist, then they are usually something that the practitioner is healing within themselves.

Q. How is it possible for the practitioner to experience the client's symptoms?

A. During a Reiki session the energy within the client and the practitioner become one. This means that if the client's mind is overactive, the practitioner's mind will also have a tendency to become overactive. Should the client be depressed, the practitioner may also feel depressed. Should the client have a heart problem, the practitioner may notice his/her own heart behaving strangely. Not every single symptom will be picked up by the practitioner, but only those symptoms that the energy feels is important for the practitioner to be aware of.

Sometimes symptoms are felt by the practitioner that the client is unaware of. I once treated a woman who had fallen down the stairs the previous night in her sleep, and during the Reiki session I felt quite nauseous. I informed her of this after our session and told her that she was in shock and that she should go home to bed. She insisted that she was perfectly alright. One hour later she became aware that she was indeed feeling shocked and nauseous and remained like this for 24 hours. She informed me afterwards that she was brought up to be stoic and that it was very difficult for her to feel any weakness in herself.

The process of the practitioner feeling the client's symptoms is called *melding*. No long term disease or dysfunction can be picked up by the practitioner. For example, if a client comes to the practitioner with arthritis of his or her back, the practitioner may feel the pain in his/her back for a few minutes during the treatment, but will not go on to develop arthritis as a result of giving the treatment.

Q. How many treatments are needed in order to alleviate a client's symptoms?
A. Generally speaking, the longer a pathology or condition has existed, the longer it takes to correct it. When Reiki is given immediately after an accident has occurred, for instance, provided no bones are broken, it alleviates the condition immediately. However, when the condition has been there for six or seven days, it will take approximately six treatments to heal. When chronic conditions are treated, i.e., those conditions that have existed in the body for longer than three months, they will take longer to heal. In such instances it is recommended that the client receives four consecutive sessions, preferably one each day, then two sessions per week for four weeks, and then, if the client needs further treatment, once a week. At this stage he/she may decide to do a Reiki course and treat him/her self or continue to visit the practitioner on a weekly basis as well as treating him/her self daily. For chronic conditions, it is

impossible to say exactly how long it will take to alleviate the symptoms.

One of my client's had a bowel problem for ten years. She decided to take a Reiki course and treated herself for three hours each day and after a month of doing this, she was completely healed of all her symptoms. For chronic conditions it may vary from months to years in order to achieve a complete alleviation of the symptoms and the disease may always remain within the body. The emotional and spiritual healing that occurs with Reiki is as important as the physical healing when it comes to chronic conditions. Very early on in the treatment process, clients feel happier and more peaceful. This internal peace seems to be a major catalyst in helping chronic sufferers to cope with pain and also to release the disease.

Q. Is there any danger involved in treating someone else or myself with Reiki?
A. A few points that are very important when treating people with Reiki:
a. Never treat without a medical diagnosis
The reason for this is simple – you do not know what it is that you are treating. For example, if someone comes to you with back pain, this could be caused by something as simple as a strained muscle or a kidney infection, but it could also be caused by a tumour somewhere in the spine. A qualified medical practitioner is the only person with the education and diagnostic tools to decide what the cause of the pain is. While Reiki will be helpful in all these conditions, in certain situations, orthodox medicine might be essential. For example Reiki might work to remove a tumour but it would take longer to do so than surgery during which time the tumour might have caused permanent nerve damage or in certain

31

areas of the body might have caused death. Once the diagnosis is received, there are three choices available to the client. Orthodox medicine only, alternative medicine or a combination of both. The choice can only be made on accurate information and by analysing the advantages and disadvantages of both.

b. Do not treat severely mentally ill clients
Treating mentally ill clients or clients who are on medication that affects the chemistry of the brain is not recommended. The reason for this is that the first three treatments can exaggerate the symptoms and the client might damage him/her self. For example, if someone is schizophrenic with manic periods, their mania may become more pronounced leading to dangerous activities such as jumping off a tall building in an effort to fly. They should only be treated in a controlled environment. A practitioner would need to be working in a hospital in order to treat clients with severe mental problems. It is perfectly safe to treat clients with mild reactive depression or with slight dementia.

c. Do not treat women in the first three months of pregnancy
The Reiki energy always works for the good of the person but if the woman should miscarry her child there is no way of proving that this was not caused by Reiki. Miscarriages occur most commonly during the first three months. Where there is no danger of litigation it is perfectly safe to Reiki the pregnant mother in the first three months of pregnancy.

d. Do not treat someone without giving them details of Reiki generally and their treatment specifically
When one is working with Reiki, responsibility should always be given to the client for his/her session. This is

because an intimate connection is formed with the client, and if this feels uncomfortable for the client in any way, it is up to the client to inform the practitioner. This arises especially in cases where there is a history of abuse in the client or where the client may feel uncomfortable when touched on certain parts of the body.

When the client first arrives, explain Reiki to him/her. Then give the client an article on Reiki and ask him/her to read it before attending the next session. On his/her arrival for the second session, enquire whether there are any questions about Reiki, either about the article or his/her experience following his/her initial Reiki session.

Immediately before the client lies down to receive their initial Reiki session, outline to him/her exactly what is involved. For example: *For your Reiki session you will be lying down and you will have a blanket over you. I will place my hands on your body going through a sequence of positions, staying in each position for three or four minutes. Should you be uncomfortable with my hands anywhere please let me know and I will move them on to a new position. Before I begin, is there any place on your body where you are not comfortable being touched?* This makes it clear to the client beforehand that it is perfectly acceptable if he/she does not want certain parts of his/her body to be touched. It also places the responsibility onto the client that if he/she is uncomfortable with the experience of being touched in any area then he/she can ask that this position be omitted. It is impossible for the practitioner to identify during the treatment if the client has a problem with being touched on any part of the body.

Then go on to discuss the effect of Reiki generally. To do this, give the following information. *In this treatment your body will absorb energy from the air through my body which will act as a conductor of this energy. During the entire treatment your body will control the energy, its intensity, its frequency and what it does with that energy. You will experience the energy by feeling relaxed, and you may also fall asleep. You may notice a feeling of warmth or coolness where I touch you and there may be a tingling underneath my hands. Occasionally people experience a feeling of being rocked or moved, and if this happens it is just the energy moving inside your body. The treatment is done mostly in silence, but if there is anything that you feel is important to discuss, please feel free to interrupt.*

It is important to emphasise to the client that it is his/her treatment and as such, it can be interrupted and renewed at any time. People who hold a lot of fear in their body may experience a panic attack during the Reiki session, and it is important that these people feel comfortable in stopping the practitioner before the attack reaches a crisis point. Other clients may become very chilled or overheated during a Reiki session and it is important that these clients understand that the blanket or the temperature of the room can be adjusted to suit their needs.

Q. How do I interpret the sensations in my hands in relation to what is happening to the client?
A. There is an array of sensations you can feel in the hands, and you soon discover that a certain sensation very often means a particular condition is present in the client's tissues. If you sense that nothing at all is happening, this generally means that the client's tissues are not taking much energy. This is especially true if you notice that Reiki is not flowing through your body.

Sometimes the practitioner may not notice much energy flowing in his/her own hands, but will notice energy flowing in his/her body. This means that the client is receiving energy.

The temperature of the practitioner's hands may change giving rise to either a sensation of warmth or coldness. This is an indication that energy is flowing.

There may be tingling in the practitioner's fingers and hands. This usually occurs in the first few months following Reiki training and this indicates that the practitioner's channels are opening up and becoming more available.

Sometimes a pulse is felt in the client's tissue beneath the practitioner's hands. This indicates that the tissue here is healing and that the client's energy pathways are re-opening in that particular area of the body. This is known as the therapeutic pulse.

Sharp pains, either in the hands themselves, or shooting up the practitioner's arms that exit at the elbow joint or shoulder joints indicates the release of swelling in the client's tissues. This is mostly felt when there is swelling of the nerve tissue.

Sometimes the energy oscillates in a continuous motion from one of the practitioner's hands to the other. This usually means that a large area of tissue is affected, and trapped energy is releasing.

Occasionally a practitioner will feel nauseous treating a client. This usually means that toxins of some kind are present throughout the client's whole body. The practitioner may want to treat such a client for shorter periods. Nausea can also be an indication of emotional blockages in the client, especially in the abdominal area.

The practitioner should be aware of his/her own emotional, mental and spiritual states so that he/she can distinguish between those which belong to the practitioner and those which belong to the client.

Q. Do I have to give a complete treatment every time?
A. No, not necessarily. *Some Reiki is better than none.* For

chronic illnesses, it is better to treat the whole body. For localised aches and pains it is sufficient to treat the effected area alone.

When there is a localised condition, e.g., a broken ankle, it is appropriate to work on that area only. At other times the practitioner may work on three or four different areas, e.g., for sinus problems, use the head positions.

You should always remember that pain can be referred. This means that the cause of pain and the experience of it, may be in two different places in the body. This is one of the main reasons why the client should always be seen by a medical practitioner before being treated by a Reiki practitioner. The most common sites of referred pain are:

ORIGIN	SITE OF REFERRAL
Heart	Chest and left arm
Abdominal pain	Left shoulder
Neck	Arms, head or lower back
Lower back	Pelvis, hips and legs

When pain is referred, it is best to treat both the site of the pain and the origin of the pain.

Q. Why do I feel shy about doing Reiki on somebody else?
A. Most of us feel uncomfortable touching other people and especially touching people whom we have never met before. A practitioner may feel very uncomfortable touching a client early on following Reiki training. It takes a little while to become accustomed to touching other people, particularly people you do not know and especially members of the opposite sex. However, the more Reiki treatments a practitioner gives, the more

natural touching the client will become. The client very often does not feel the practitioner's hands but is simply aware of the energy flowing in his/her own body. A practitioner should remember that it is natural to feel uncomfortable touching a client in the early stages of practising Reiki, but that gradually you will become accustomed to it and your embarrassment falls away as you realise that your touch is assisting the client.

Q. What happens if I cannot give four consecutive treatments?
A. The ideal situation is to have the client receive four treatments consecutively – one treatment a day. However, for various reasons it is not always possible for this to happen. As stated previously, *some Reiki is better than none*, so if the client can only come to one, two or perhaps three treatments, the client will still benefit. Sometimes it is necessary to space the treatments further apart and whilst the response is not always as dramatic as if the treatments were closer together, the Reiki is still beneficial to the client.

Q. Can Reiki be used on a dying person?
A. Reiki is a marvellous tool to assist a person in the process of transition from one dimension of reality to another. Reiki is useful on the physical level in assisting the alleviation of pain. Reiki assists the person mentally by helping to calm the person's mind and to assist him/her in focusing on completing that which needs completing before the end of his/her life on earth. On an emotional level Reiki brings a person to a place of peace and oneness, which is necessary if that person is to let go of this life, and move on to the next. Reiki, however, is most beneficial to a dying person on the spiritual level as it brings in spiritual energy to the person while they

are still on the physical plane, so when they move on to a completely spiritual way of being, the journey is much shorter and there is less shock to the soul. It is also beneficial for the family of the dying person to practise Reiki on his/her family members. It removes a sense of helplessness and gives the practitioner a sense of involvement in the death process, so that his/her role is an active one as opposed to a passive one. Of course Reiki may be combined with prayer and meditation, and it brings out in the dying person, and his or her friends and family, a spiritual dimension which is so often lacking in our day to day lives.

Finally it gives a practitioner more insight into what the dying person is experiencing. A practitioner recounted to me how, after she had spent many hours at her dying mother's bedside, she had to visit her daughter who lived 150 miles away. On arrival at her daughter's home, she had a premonition that her mother needed assistance and immediately telephoned the nursing staff at the hospital requesting that her mother be checked. She then sent her mother some long-distance energy and while doing this she received a vision of two angels and Jesus coming down over her mother's bed, and of her mother stretching her arms up toward them. A few minutes later the hospital telephoned to inform her that her mother had just died. Experiences similar to this are not unusual when using Reiki with dying people.

Q. How long is best to work on myself each day?
A. You should work on yourself for a minimum of 20 minutes each day – five minutes on the pelvis, five minutes on the abdomen, five minutes on the chest and five minutes on the head. This treats all the main organs and glands in the body. However, if there is a weakness in any particular area of the body, it is preferable to stay

working on that area until the energy here balances with the energy in the rest of the body. The longer you spend Reikiing yourself, the healthier you will become. There is no danger of over-treating yourself.

Q. When is the best time to Reiki myself?
A. The body is most receptive to Reiki when it is warm and relaxed. The body takes in more Reiki just before you get out of bed in the morning than at any other time. It also takes in considerable amounts of energy when you wake up during the night. Every time you wake up, place your hands on yourself wherever you feel energy is needed. You can Reiki yourself anywhere – sitting in a chair, chatting, reading a book, watching television or a video or at a concert.

Q. Can I give myself too much Reiki?
A. No, the more energy you have the more you can achieve in life. When I am on holiday, I Reiki myself for about three hours daily, to make up for the years I did not Reiki myself. One of my practitioners had a cyst on one of her ovaries, and was scheduled for surgery. She Reikied her ovary for sixteen hours a day for two days, and the cyst was re-absorbed and the surgery cancelled. There is no danger of over-treating yourself and only good comes from Reiki.

Q. Will Reiki help me to sleep?
A. For most people Reiki has a relaxing, sedative effect and assists in promoting sleep. Some people find that Reiki acts as a stimulant and those people should Reiki themselves in the morning only. A practitioner has reported that Reikiing herself in bed kept her husband awake, and he requested that she *turn herself off* when he was in bed with her. One must also take into consideration

the effect it may have on your partner.

Q. How will Reiki I affect my life?

A. The following are the changes experienced following Level I.

a. *Increased sensitivity* to alcohol, drugs, sugar and medication – as much smaller amounts of these substances now achieve the same effect as a larger amount would have previously.

b. *Increased intuition.*

c. *Heightened dream life* – more colour, shape and information in dreams than previously experienced.

d. *Greater physical safety*, even to the extent that inanimate objects, such as cars, behave in such a way as to keep the practitioner safe.

e. A greater *feeling of oneness* with children, plants, animals and nature. It, as it were, cracks the code on life and reduces separation.

f. A tendency towards *vegetarianism.*

g. *Greater impact in life*, both personally and professionally.

i. *Some changes in heart beat* may be noticed since the Reiki strengthens the heart as it passes through to the hands. These changes can occur even when the practitioner is not practising Reiki.

CHAPTER 6

Hand Positions in Reiki

REIKI HAND POSITIONS WHILE LYING DOWN

The first five positions are done with the practitioner sitting at the head of the client with the client lying on his/her back.

Figure 1

POSITION 1

The first hand position is at the back of the head with the tips of the fingers extending down onto the neck. This position is good for eye problems, headaches, hay fever, sinuses, indigestion, shock, and sorrow. It has a relaxing effect on the client and helps to clear excessive thoughts from the mind. It is known as the master position because by treating this position in a client, it has an overflow effect and treats every other part of the body.

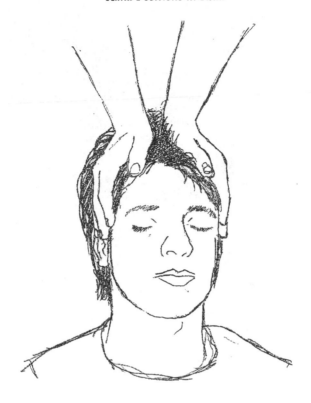

Figure 2

POSITION 2

This position is known as the 'hair band' position because the hands are placed in a similar position to a hair band on the head. The wrists meet at the crown of the head and the hands are placed in opposite directions down towards the client's ears. There is a gap of about 1cm between the wrists at the top of the head. This position treats the pineal and pituitary gland. It treats the brain and it also treats the seventh chakra. It is useful for symptoms such as headaches, eye problems, difficulties with movement that have a neurological background and also, on an emotional level, it has a calming effect.

43

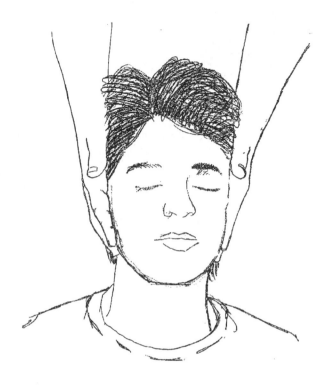

Figure 3

POSITION 3

Position 3 is when the hands cover the ears with the fingers extended down towards the neck. It is really a continuation of position 2. This position is useful in treating any imbalances between both sides of the brain. It is useful in treating hearing problems and also for any memory difficulties. It treats the ears where there are acupuncture points which affect every other part of the body. When we work on this position, we also assist in healing the entire body.

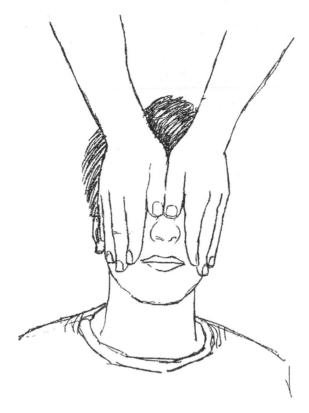

Figure 4

POSITION 4

In this position, the wrists and palms of the hands are resting on the front of the head and forehead with the fingers extending down over the eyes. This position treats the eyes, the front of the brain, the front of the sinuses and the sixth chakra. It also treats the pituitary gland which is responsible for the glands all over the body.

Sinus problems are very common in this age of air pollution. I have achieved good results using the above four positions, holding each one for 15 minutes.

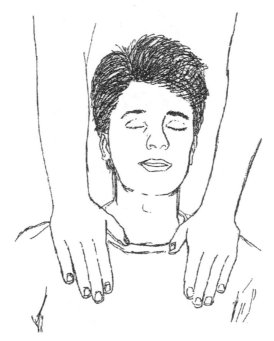

Figure 5

POSITION 5

Position 5 treats the neck, throat and thyroid gland. It is very important to avoid putting direct pressure on the throat as this could alter the clients breathing and blood pressure and may be very distressing for the client.

There are two ways of treating the neck. One way is to treat the neck from the front by placing the hands on the client's collar bone and first ribs. This position is used to treat thyroid problems, throat problems and infections in the body. When the client is suffering from headaches or from any orthopaedic problems in the neck, it is best to treat the neck from the back. This is done by slipping your hands in at the back of the neck. This position helps to relieve headaches as well as any neck problems.

46

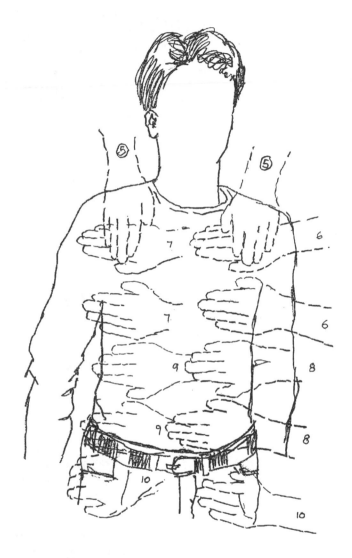

Figure 6

POSITIONS 6 TO 12
These positions are carried out while sitting or standing at the client's side.

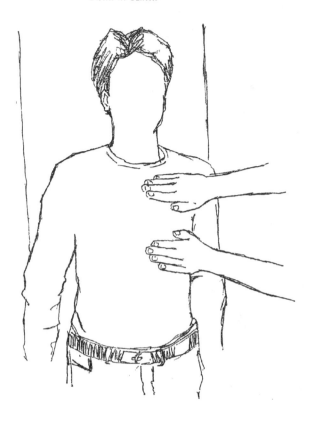

Figure 7

POSITION 6

Position 6 treats the heart, left lung and thymus gland. The uppermost hand is placed close to the left shoulder and the lower hand is placed below the left breast. The heart is a very vulnerable area and it should be touched with great sensitivity and awareness, as there is a large amount of stored emotional energy around the heart. The heart usually takes in a considerable amount of energy because of its emotional and physical importance in the body, and a practitioner often needs to spend a few extra minutes in this treatment position.

48

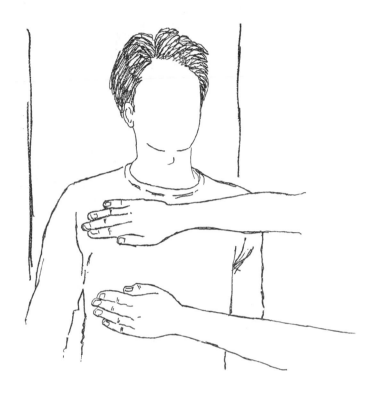

Figure 8

POSITION 7

Position 7 treats the right lung and the upper section of the liver. The uppermost hand is placed close to the right shoulder and the lower hand is placed just below the right breast. When working with women, it is very important not to touch the breast directly except in cases where there is a specific problem with the breast. It is also necessary to inform the client before the treatment that you wish to place your hand on the breast, and to obtain permission to do so.

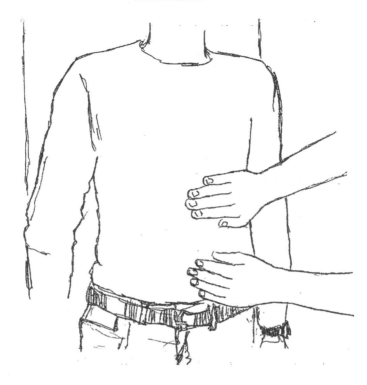

Figure 9

POSITION 8

In this position the uppermost hand is placed just below the ribcage, and the lower hand is placed 2cm below it. This position treats the stomach, colon, spleen, liver, pancreas, small intestines, reproductive organs and the bladder. It is used to treat stomach problems, digestive problems, hypoglycaemia, diabetes, problems with the immune system and emotional problems such as shock, depression, fear, anger or resentment. It is also used to treat problems with the reproductive system and the bladder.

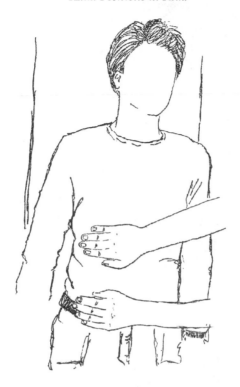

Figure 10

POSITION 9

In this position the uppermost hand is placed just below the ribcage and the lower hand about 2cm below it on the left hand side of the body. This position treats the large and small intestines, reproductive system and the bladder, gallstones and hepatitis. It is also used for any problems in the digestive or reproductive system. It is important to remember that the appendix is found on the right hand side of the body and you must always be wary of pain in this area in case the client is experiencing an attack of acute appendicitis. This position also treats any emotional problems when it is combined with position 8.

51

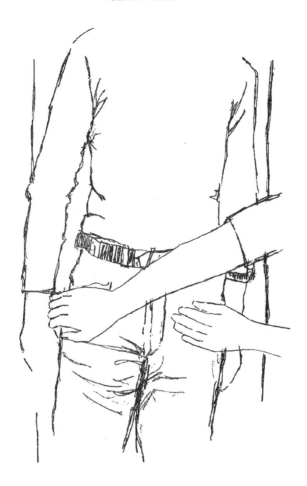

Figure 11

POSITION 10

Position 10 treats the groins, hip joints and circulation to the legs and lymph nodes. This position is very important in treating a person's physical vitality through its affect on the first chakra.

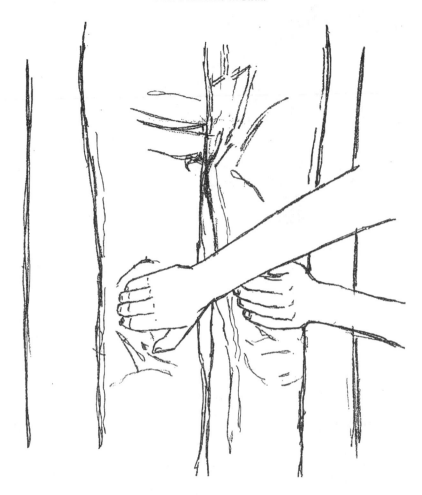

Figure 12

POSITION 11

Position 11 treats the knees. It is sufficient to place one hand on each knee. This position treats any physical problems in the knee joint as well as promoting flexibility and grounding. Once again this position can be carried out with the practitioner sitting or standing beside the client.

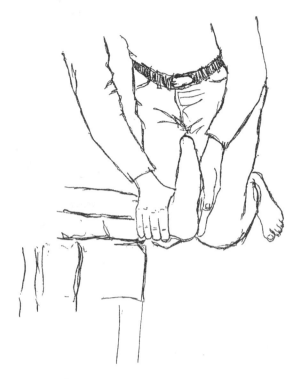

Figure 13

POSITION 12

The twelfth position treats the feet. It is performed by placing the uppermost hand across the ankle joint and the lower hand along the sole of the client's foot. This position promotes circulation to the feet and relieves any orthopaedic problems in this area. It helps to ground the client too and, because all the organs have an energy connection with the soles of the feet, it helps to heal the entire body.

The following positions are carried out with the client lying face downwards.

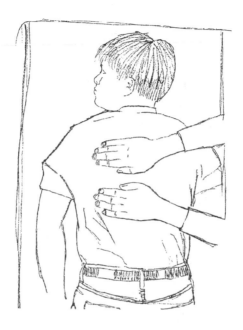

Figure 14

POSITION 13

Position 13 requires one hand to be placed above the client's left shoulder blade and the practitioner's other hand placed below the client's left shoulder blade. This position treats the client's left shoulder, left lung and the back of the heart. Most people have extremely tight musculature here because, on an unconscious level, a fear of betrayal may be held in this part of the body. The back of the heart, just like the front, absorbs a considerable amount of energy. This energy is directed solely towards the client, as opposed to assisting the client to nurture other people, which occurs when energy is received in the front of the heart.

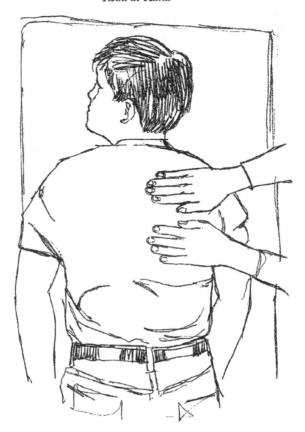

Figure 15

POSITION 14

In this position one of the practitioner's hands is placed on the back of the client's right shoulder and the other hand is placed immediately below the shoulder blade. This position treats the right lung and the nerve supply to the right arm and right lung. Positions 13 and 14 are used to relieve stress, sleeplessness, anxiety and nervousness. On a physical level, positions 13 and 14 are used to treat any lung, heart or liver problems.

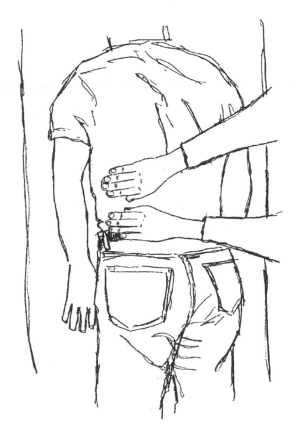

Figure 16

POSITION 15

In position 15 the practitioner has one hand just below the client's ribcage and the other hand just above the buttock area. This position treats the client's left kidney, lumber spine area and the back of the abdomen. In this position, the client will also absorb a considerable amount of energy as the adrenal glands, which are situated on top of the kidneys, assist in supplying the body with energy. This position is used to treat back pain, allergies, stress, shock, and assists in detoxification.

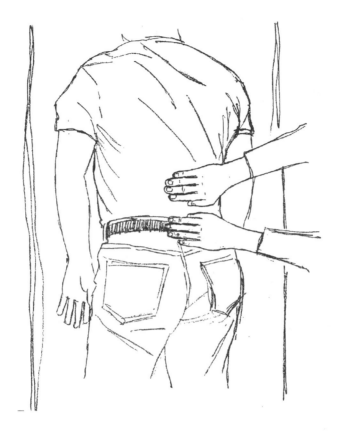

Figure 17

POSITION 16

In position 16 the practitioner has his/her hands in the same positions as in position 15, except they are on the right hand side of the body. This position treats the right kidney, lumber spine and abdominal area. It also treats the back of the liver. On an anatomical level this is the weakest part of the spine and the most common site of pain. It is because of this weakness and the presence of the kidneys here that a considerable amount of energy is absorbed by the client in positions 15 and 16.

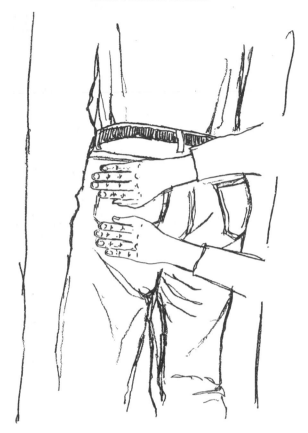

Figure 18

POSITION 17

Here, the practitioner's hands are placed on the client's buttocks on the left hand side of the body. This position treats the pelvis which contains the reproductive organs, bowel and bladder. It also treats the tail bone, the muscles to the tail bone, the left hip, and the sciatic nerve which runs through this area from the lumbar spine to the client's leg. Tension is often felt here and this tension creates weakness in the lower back.

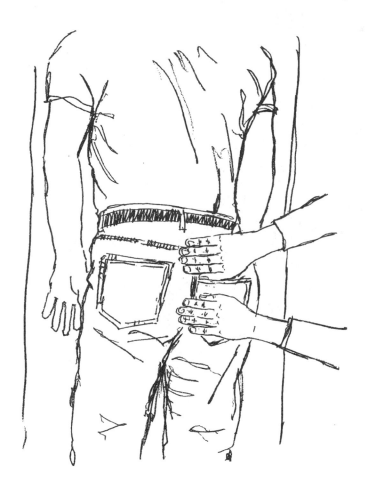

Figure 19

POSITION 18

This position shows the practitioner's hands in the same location as in position 17 except they are on the right side. It is used for the same reasons as position 17.

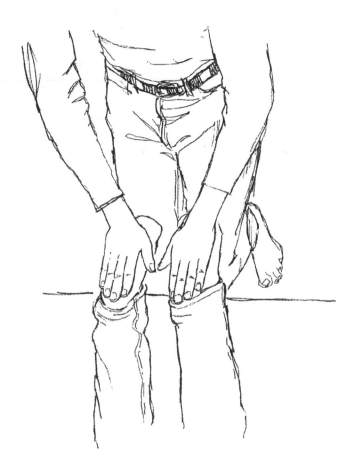

Figure 20

POSITION 19

This final position demonstrates the practitioner treating the soles of the feet with the client lying on his/her stomach. Here we see the practitioner sitting with both his/her hands resting on the soles of the client's feet. This position is used to energise the client's whole body and to ground the client.

GIVING A COMPLETE REIKI SESSION

Each position is held for four minutes and each treatment will take approximately one hour and 20 minutes. Afterwards, it is important to leave a few minutes to exchange information with the client, so it is best to leave one-and-a-half hours for a complete treatment.

During the session, the practitioner notices where the energy is flowing, both in him/her self and in the client. The practitioner also notices any strong or repeated sensations within him/her self, any visual effects, thoughts or sounds and afterwards, if the practitioner considers it relevant to the treatment, discusses them with the client.

Once, whilst treating a young man, I felt nauseous for the first 10 minutes. Afterwards, I discussed this experience with him, and he then informed me that just before coming for his Reiki treatment he had experienced something that *he could not stomach.*

The practitioner may choose to start with the client lying on his/her front or back. It might be simpler to start with the client lying on his/her stomach as this position demands more negotiation between the client and the practitioner to achieve the most comfortable position for the client. When the client has had his/her back treated and he/she is quite relaxed it is very simple for him/her to turn over on to his/her back and the treatment can be resumed with the minimum of disturbance. The feet are almost always treated at the end of a Reiki session and they need only be done once, with the client lying on either his/her front or back. If the client is very emotionally disturbed or finds it difficult to relax, it may be advisable to start on the feet and work up the body, as this helps to ground the client.

Sometimes a practitioner may choose to treat a client while he/she is sitting instead of lying down. This may be due to the shortage of a table or the client may be more comfortable in a sitting position. The following illustrations demonstrate hand positions when the client is sitting down.

REIKI HAND POSITIONS WHEN THE CLIENT IS SEATED

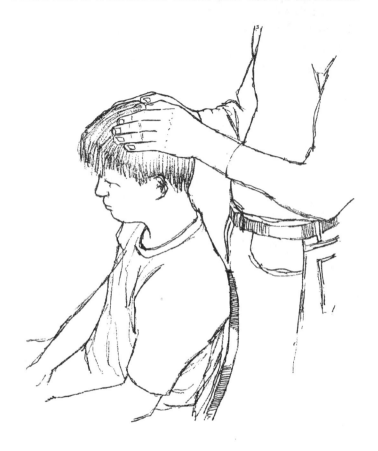

Figure 21

POSITION 1
In this position the practitioner's hands are placed on top of the client's head. This sends energy to the whole of the nervous system.

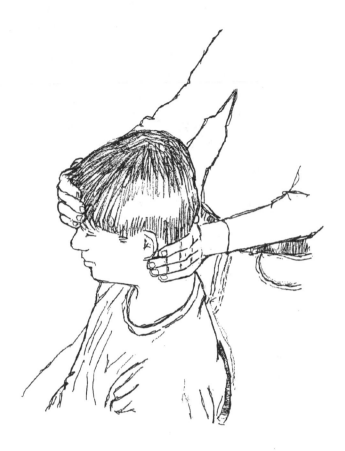

Figure 22

POSITION 2

As you can see, one of the practitioner's hands is placed
on the forehead and the other hand is placed at the base
of the client's skull at the back of the head. This position
balances the energy in the brain, and treats the pituitary
and pineal glands. It is especially useful for treating
headaches. The practitioner stands beside the client.

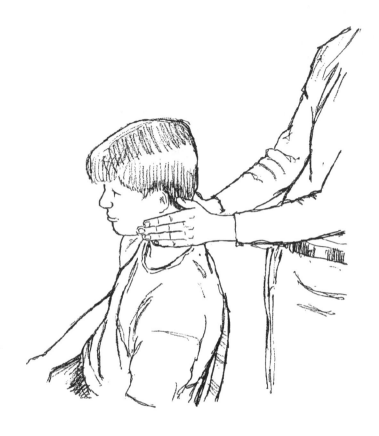

Figure 23

POSITION 3

Position 3 shows the practitioner's hands at either side of the client's neck. This position treats the neck and it is also useful for treating headaches as well as neck pain.

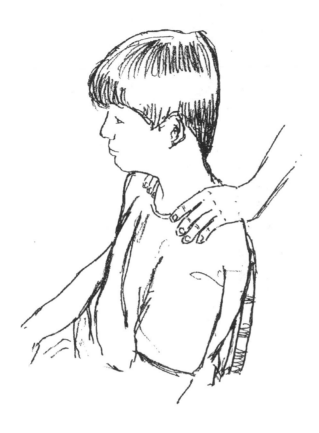

Figure 24

POSITION 4

Position 4 shows the practitioner's hands resting on the client's shoulders. This position will relax and energise the client's neck and shoulder muscles. It counteracts any inflammation in the neck and shoulder areas and also has an energising effect on the client's lungs.

67

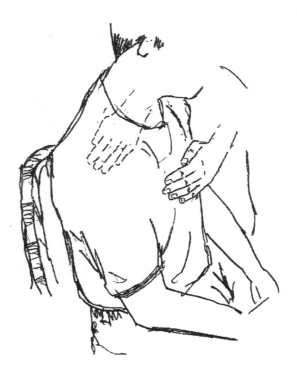

Figure 25

POSITION 5

Position 5 shows the practitioner treating the client's heart by placing one hand in front of the client's chest and the other on the back. Here the practitioner is sitting beside the client.

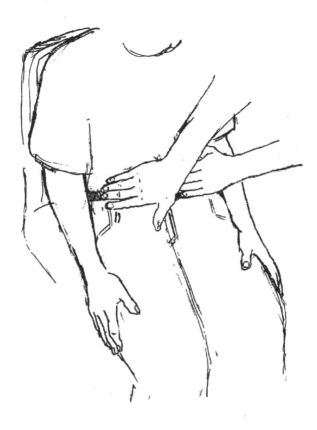

Figure 26

POSITION 6

You can treat the abdominal area by sitting beside the client and leaning forwards. However, this can be uncomfortable on the practitioner's back so, unless there is a specific abdominal problem, it is best to avoid this position. The client can be treated instead while they are lying on a kitchen table or on a bed, with the practitioner kneeling alongside.

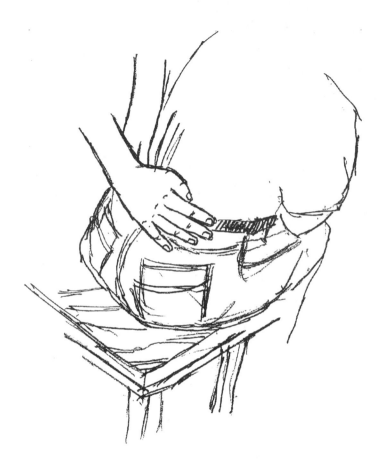

Figure 27

POSITION 7

To treat the lower back, the client needs to be sitting on a stool and the practitioner needs to stand behind the client and place his/her hands on the client's back.

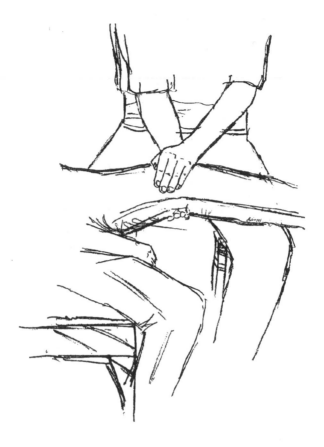

Figure 28

POSITION 8

To treat the client's knees while sitting, the practitioner needs to sit beside the client with the client's leg lying across the practitioner's thighs. The practitioner then places one hand below the knee and the other above the knee. To treat the other knee, the practitioner simply moves his/her chair to the other side of the client and repeats the procedure.

71

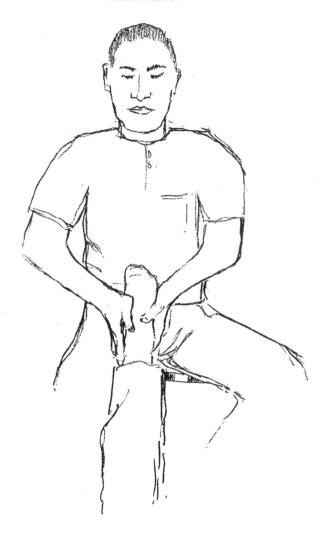

Figure 29

POSITION 9

To treat a client's feet or ankles, the client places his/her foot on the practitioner's thighs, and the practitioner places his/her hands at either side of the ankle or foot.

SELF-TREATMENT

Finally we come to self-treatment. This is the most important of all because to understand how Reiki works on others you need to experience it on yourself. Reiki is a very powerful healing force and if you treat yourself on a daily basis for 20 minutes or so, it is unlikely that you will become seriously ill. The body is most receptive to energy when it is warm and relaxed, and this is usually at night in bed or first thing in the morning before getting out of bed. However, remember that no concentration is necessary when treating yourself, and you may treat yourself while watching television, a show or when you are chatting to friends. It is possible to treat oneself even when reading a book – holding the book with one hand and Reikiing oneself with the other! Once Reiki is learned, you will find that you cannot keep your hands off yourself!

Positions 1 to 4 are recommended as daily treatment, as they cover all the major organs and glands in the body. Positions 5 to 7 need only be practised as the need arises.

Positions 1 to 7 shown with the practitioner lying down, can also be performed whilst sitting

Figure 30

POSITION 1

The practitioner places his/her right hand on the right hand side of the pelvis quite close to the centre, on the right, and the left hand on the left side.

Figure 31

POSITION 2

The upper abdominal and lower chest area is most comfortably treated by placing the hands across the body, and treating the left side with the right hand and the right side with the left hand. Rest the hands on the upper abdominal, lower ribcage area.

75

Figure 32

POSITION 3

The upper chest and heart is most easily treated by crossing the hands on the chest, and resting them on the upper chest and collar bone area.

Figure 33

POSITION 4

The head can be treated by placing both hands behind the head or one hand at the back of your head and the other hand on your forehead, or both hands on the front of the head. No matter which position you choose, it still puts a strain on your arms to have them stretched above shoulder level. This discomfort is best alleviated by placing two pillows beneath your arms so that they are well supported.

77

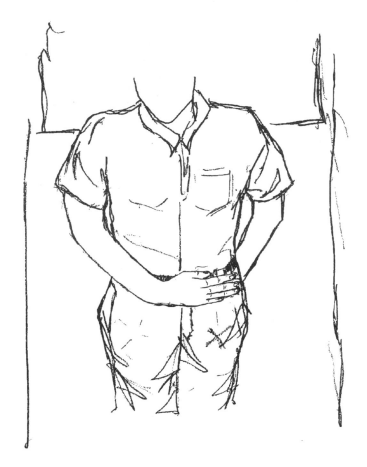

Figure 34

POSITION 5

The hips are treated by placing one hand beneath the hip and the other in the groin area. This can be done when you are either sitting or lying down.

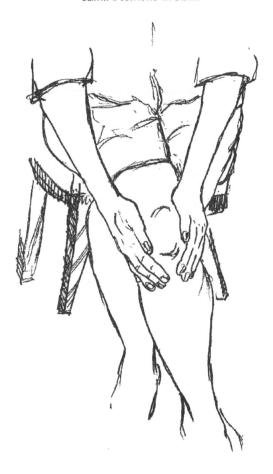

Figure 35

POSITION 6

It is easier to treat the knee while sitting. Cross one leg over the other, taking care not to put any pressure on the back of the knee as this may impede circulation. Place a hand at either side of the uppermost leg. The knee can also be treated by lying on your side and bending the knee up towards the trunk while placing a hand at either side of the knee.

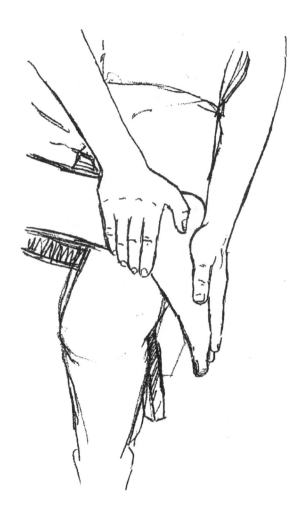

Figure 36

POSITION 7

This position demonstrates how to treat your feet while sitting down. Simply cross one leg over the other and place one hand along the sole of your foot and the other on the ankle joint.

80

CHAPTER 7

Chakras

There are seven main energy centres in the body that control the flow of energy to a being. These energy centres are known as chakras, a Sanskrit word for wheel. They are called wheels because they rotate or spin. Each chakra spins at a different frequency. The lower a chakra is in the body, the slower the rotation. Because the chakras rotate at different frequencies, they are each represented by a different colour.

The function of a chakra is to collect energy and transform it so that it may be used by the body either physically, emotionally, mentally or spiritually. The chakras run parallel to the spine. Each chakra has a gland or organ associated with it. In Reiki, we need to be aware of the physical location of each chakra and its role as Reiki works on the chakras of both the client and the practitioner. It is a good idea to balance the chakras after a Reiki session, as the client will be very relaxed and responsive. Balancing the client's chakras will enhance the effect of a treatment.

FIRST CHAKRA (THE ROOT OR BASE CHAKRA)

PHYSICAL LOCATION: The first chakra is found at the base of the spine.

COLOUR: Red.

ASSOCIATED ORGAN: Sexual organs.

FUNCTION: It grounds you, gives you physical vitality and controls your sexuality and creativity. When it is functioning optimally you are well grounded, have good physical energy and experience total well-being without stress. You are also creatively fulfilled and able to express your sexuality appropriately.

MALFUNCTIONING: This client will have difficulty grounding. When in communication with this client, the practitioner will feel drained afterwards. This client will have difficulty in holding on to finances and there will be a history of either physical or mental problems. Very often this chakra functions poorly in people who have been abused as children.

AFFIRMATION: It is safe to be in your body.

SECOND CHAKRA   (THE FEELING CHAKRA)

PHYSICAL LOCATION: The second chakra is found slightly to the left of the navel.

COLOUR: Orange.

ASSOCIATED ORGAN: Spleen.

FUNCTION: This chakra controls the feeling tones of the body and in some people it is the centre of their intuition. In Japan, this area is known as the *hara* and energy that is created in the first chakra is stored here and re-distributed throughout the body as it is required. When it is functioning optimally the client feels peaceful with themselves and the world. When they are in tune with their own needs, they will tend to act as opposed to react. They will have very good intuition and will be successful in their career. It is very pleasant to be around a person whose second chakra is working well as there are no strings attached to any interaction.

MALFUNCTIONING: When a second chakra does not work well, he/she will have considerable physical problems in this area, varying from indigestion, irritable bowel problems, ulcers, diabetes or circulatory problems. He/she may have mood swings or behave in a very demanding fashion. He/she may also have suicidal tendencies if this moodiness is turned inwards.

AFFIRMATION: It is safe to feel.

THIRD CHAKRA (THE POWER CHAKRA)

PHYSICAL LOCATION: The third chakra is found at the base of the breastbone, and it is called the power centre.

COLOUR: Yellow.

ASSOCIATED GLAND: Adrenal glands.

FUNCTION: The third chakra has to do with the logical thinking mind, will and power. When this is functioning well, the client will have a sense of pride in themselves. They make clear logical decisions, and, taking their emotional welfare into account, they set realistic goals in life and usually achieve them. Failure is not experienced as something negative, but as an opportunity to reassess goals and objectives.

MALFUNCTIONING: When a person's third chakra is not aligned correctly, there is a subconscious fear of success. The person is either uncomfortable with responsibility or will take on a considerable amount of responsibility but work with it in such a way that it is destructive for themselves and others. The latter group of people will come across as overbearing. This chakra is weak in adults who were not validated as children.

AFFIRMATION: It is safe to be powerful.

FOURTH CHAKRA (THE HEART CHAKRA)

PHYSICAL LOCATION: The fourth chakra is positioned at the centre of the heart.

COLOUR: Green.

ASSOCIATED GLAND: Thymus Gland.

FUNCTION: It controls the love we give to ourselves and others. In some people it is the centre of intuition instead of the second chakra. These people feel things in their heart before they feel them in their gut. When it is functioning well a person feels light-hearted. They feel love and compassion for themselves and others and for all situations which come into their lives. They are considered to be strong hearted. People who have the ability to see non-physical frequencies of energy tell us that the soul resides within the heart.

MALFUNCTIONING: When this chakra is not aligned properly there will be problems with the heart on a physical level. Emotionally one feels heavy-hearted. Love will be given to themselves and others in measured amounts with no sense of infinity or abundance. These people feel vulnerable to other people's moods and needs and usually create a relationship of co-dependence in order to create safety.

AFFIRMATION: It is safe to give and receive love.

FIFTH CHAKRA (THE THROAT CHAKRA)

PHYSICAL LOCATION: The fifth chakra is found in the throat and in the neck.

COLOUR: Blue.

ASSOCIATED GLAND: The thyroid.

FUNCTION: The fifth chakra controls our expression and creativity. When it functions optimally, people express their emotions and thoughts freely. They experience a quality of flexibility in their lives, adapting easily to the changing circumstances of life. The back of the throat chakra controls a telepathic centre with which one feels non-physical frequencies of energy.

MALFUNCTIONING: When this chakra closes down, people become choked up, as happens most commonly at funerals, and the Oscars! There is also a tendency to develop physical problems in the throat and neck area such as laryngitis or perhaps arthritis of the neck. This chakra is very closely associated with the second chakra.

AFFIRMATION: It is safe to express your ideas and emotions.

SIXTH CHAKRA (THE THIRD EYE CHAKRA)

PHYSICAL LOCATION: It lies in the middle of the forehead, just a little higher than the eyebrows.

COLOUR: Indigo (or the colour of the evening sky).

ASSOCIATED GLAND: Pituitary gland.

FUNCTION: When this centre is properly aligned it gives people a sense of vision of where they are going in life and how to prioritise things. It is closely associated with the third chakra. When highly developed it permits people to see non-physical frequencies of energy such as the auric field around people, or non-physical entities such as angels. Blind people very often see in colour. This is made possible through the third eye, when the physical eyes are no longer functioning properly. People with perfect sight see colours with their eyes closed – again through the third eye.

MALFUNCTIONING: When this chakra is not functioning well a person finds it difficult to see different aspects of life. They tend to have tunnel vision. They are also afraid of being in the public eye or being singled out in any way. When it is too strong, the person will be known as a dreamer. He/she will have lots of good ideas but will find it very difficult to implement them. When there is good grounding, he/she will go into organisation and get other people to follow these ideas. When the grounding is weak, however, all these great ideas go to waste as the individual does not know how to implement his/her creativity.

AFFIRMATION: It is safe to see and be seen.

SEVENTH CHAKRA (THE CROWN CHAKRA)

PHYSICAL LOCATION: The seventh chakra is found in the crown of the head.

COLOUR: Violet or purple.

ASSOCIATED GLAND: Pineal Gland.

FUNCTION: The seventh chakra is the location of union between a person's internal energy and the universal energy or God. During a Reiki workshop, this area of the body becomes extremely warm. When it is functioning well, a person experiences a sense of peace and oneness with life. There is a sense that life is a supportive experience. You are aware of the spiritual dimension of life. People living in countries like India, Burma, Ireland and Tibet have highly developed seventh chakras, as, wherever you go in these countries, statues to spiritual deities and saints are very visible and spirituality is an integral part of life there.

MALFUNCTIONING: When the seventh chakra is not properly aligned, he/she experiences a sense of isolation described by Mother Teresa as spiritual poverty. You feel you must control everything in life or you will be controlled by it. When the seventh chakra is overdeveloped he/she feels the need to be alone with their God/Goddess over the course of a lifetime. Material matters and their fellow companions are of no consequence.

AFFIRMATION: Accept your oneness with the God/Goddess and with all things.

BALANCING THE CHAKRAS

Balancing the chakras is done by placing your hand about 12cm above each chakra and silently saying the appropriate affirmation. Once the affirmation has been said, the practitioner moves on to the next chakra. It is best to start at the first chakra and move up to the seventh as energy moves upwards in the chakra system. It is important to emphasise here that in balancing the chakras, no force is ever used. You simply note how available the chakra is by the level of warmth you feel in your hand at that particular area and give the chakra permission to open or to close as it feels appropriate. For example, in someone who may have been physically abused as a child, that person may not feel it is safe to be in his/her body. Now that the person is an adult there are choices about the relationships that he/she is involved in, and it is not necessary for that person to be in an abusive relationship any longer. It is, however, necessary to update the chakra with new information – to let it know that now it is safe for this person to be in his/her body because while the person's situation in life may have changed, the subconscious thinking and the programming of the chakra may not have changed at all. Balancing the chakra encourages the chakra to change.

THE CHAKRAS

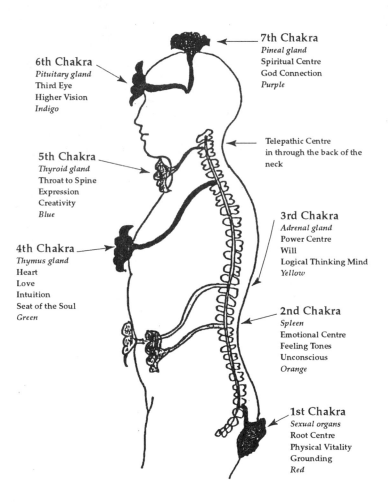

7th Chakra
Pineal gland
Spiritual Centre
God Connection
Purple

6th Chakra
Pituitary gland
Third Eye
Higher Vision
Indigo

Telepathic Centre
in through the back of the
neck

5th Chakra
Thyroid gland
Throat to Spine
Expression
Creativity
Blue

3rd Chakra
Adrenal gland
Power Centre
Will
Logical Thinking Mind
Yellow

4th Chakra
Thymus gland
Heart
Love
Intuition
Seat of the Soul
Green

2nd Chakra
Spleen
Emotional Centre
Feeling Tones
Unconscious
Orange

1st Chakra
Sexual organs
Root Centre
Physical Vitality
Grounding
Red

Figure 37

CHAPTER 8

Guidelines for Reiki Treatments

To summarise what we have learned about giving a Reiki treatment: before the client arrives, bless the room. At Level II a symbol is given to the practitioner to bless the room, but at the Level I stage, the practitioner can choose his/her own method of doing it. For example, the room may be prepared for a treatment by burning a candle, placing a bunch of flowers or sacred object in it, saying a prayer or doing a visualisation or meditation of some kind. This creates an atmosphere of healing which the client will perceive on a conscious or subconscious level once he/she enters the room. The practitioner should wash his/her hands before the client arrives and remove his/her jewellery so as not to injure the client with any sharp edges. The practitioner's hands and wrists may swell up whilst channelling Reiki. Wedding bands do not have to be removed.

It is also helpful to place a combination of hand cream and essential lavender oil on the practitioner's hands. Lavender oil will help to balance the client's emotions and counteract any lingering odours on the practitioner's hands. The client should be informed that the practitioner is using the oil to ensure that he/she does not object, and is aware of the source of the smell.

On the client's first visit, the practitioner should

discuss his/her reason for choosing a Reiki treatment. If there is a medical problem, the practitioner should establish a clear understanding of its history. If necessary ask the client to visit an orthodox medical practitioner for an assessment and diagnosis if they have not already done so. This is very important because Reiki will not work quickly enough to alleviate some problems and another form of treatment may be more appropriate. This is the case, for example, with acute appendicitis, where surgical intervention is necessary and certainly more appropriate than Reiki. When a practitioner treats a client without the benefit of an orthodox diagnosis, the practitioner is endangering him/her self by behaving in a negligent fashion. Without knowing all the facts the practitioner could be endangering the life of the client. Once a client has received the diagnosis, then the client and the practitioner are aware of exactly what they are working with, and can make an informed treatment choice. Sometimes orthodox medicine alone is appropriate, sometimes Reiki alone is appropriate, and sometimes a combination of the two is best. This decision can only be made when all the facts are known.

A general explanation of Reiki is then given to the client similar to the one on pages 33 and 34 and the client is given a specific explanation of a Reiki treatment. It is useful to inform the client that it is his/her body that controls the amount and distribution of energy throughout the session. It is also important to inform the client at this stage that there may be a worsening of his/her condition during the first three or four Reiki sessions before an improvement in symptoms is noticeable. This is due to the healing crisis effect. A healing crisis makes symptoms more pronounced, before clearing them from the body. This is due to an increase in the blood flow to the area being worked on, resulting in increased pressure on the tissue, in order to cleanse it. The client and the practitioner are now ready to proceed with the first Reiki treatment.

The client either lies or sits comfortably. It is best that the client does not cross his or her legs, as this slows the flow of energy. A client may cross his/her arms but when the practitioner gets to this area of the body the client should be asked to simply uncross them. Music may be played during the Reiki session. This is an individual decision on the part of the client or the practitioner. A treatment is done mainly without conversation but the client should be made aware that if he/she is uncomfortable during the treatment, he/she may interrupt the session, resolve the problem and then resume treatment. The client should also be informed that it is perfectly acceptable if he/she goes to sleep. In this manner the client will absorb more energy as his/her mind will be still and relaxed. The practitioner may balance the chakras when the Reiki treatment is completed.

AFTER A REIKI TREATMENT

The client is informed that the treatment is over, and allowed to rest for a few minutes before getting off the treatment table. Once the client is sitting up, he/she can be offered a glass of water to drink as usually his/her mouth will feel quite dry. Drinking water will help the detoxification process. The client is then offered the opportunity to share anything he/she experienced during the session. The practitioner then gives feedback of his/her experience. It is important not to say too much, as Reiki continues to work on the client for some hours after the session, and the client is best left in a relaxed and quiet state.

The client is reminded that his/her reflexes may not be as fast as usual and that his/her perceptions may be slightly altered because of their relaxed state. He/she may need to proceed with a little more caution than usual, to their next destination.

GENERAL POINTS ON REIKI

1. Reiki is not a substitute for medical care but enhances it.

2. Reiki works in conjunction with other alternative healing methods, i.e., acupuncture, massage, homeopathy, etc.

3. Reiki is not recommended for use on pregnant mothers during the first three months of pregnancy and clients with psychotic problems (see page 32).

4. The more a practitioner uses Reiki the stronger the Reiki becomes.

CHAPTER 9

The Practitioner's Lifestyle

Traditionally, one of the professions with the shortest life expectancy is that of a physician. This should remind us that nurturing other people can be a very risky business, unless we are willing to take and make time to look after ourselves. Just as there are four aspects to Reiki there are also four aspects to our lives and we should ensure that we are looking after ourselves on all four counts.

SPIRITUAL NOURISHMENT
People who consciously nurture spiritual energy achieve far more in life with less effort because they come from a place of inner peace. This energy is nurtured by taking time to quiet the mind and listen to the soul. The way this is achieved is different for everybody. For some people it involves prayer, for others it involves meditation, and yet others find spiritual nourishment by working in the garden or being with friends. Reikiing yourself is a spiritual practice. It doesn't matter where spiritual nourishment comes from, as long as one consciously takes the time to develop the spiritual aspect of oneself every day. Spiritual nourishment is placed at the top of the list because spiritual attunement with your life can compensate for a loss of other aspects or deficiencies.

EMOTIONAL NOURISHMENT

We are born to be happy. Happiness is something that needs to be cultivated and the best way to cultivate happiness is by finding something that you love to do, and to put an hour a day aside to do it. After all, you deserve some reward for all your hard work.

PHYSICAL NOURISHMENT

We are primarily a physical unit and as such the body needs to be nourished on a physical level. This is achieved by the following:

1. Eating nourishing food;
2. Detoxifying your system regularly;
3. Exercising every day;
4. Bathing in aromatherapy oils;
5. Massaging your feet;
6. Reikiing yourself for 20 minutes every day, and
7. Getting sufficient rest.

MENTAL NOURISHMENT

In most philosophies there is the concept that *we are what we think* or that *we create our own reality by our thoughts*. It is necessary to keep your mind in a positive frame and to become aware of your own thinking pattern and belief system. This is achieved by listening to spiritual tapes, reading books or spending time with people who are love based as opposed to fear based. Finally, remember your dreams. Dreams are a direct access to your own subconscious. The dream state becomes heightened following Reiki training. Dreams, therefore, can give very valuable insight into what is important in your life at different times.

CHAPTER 10

The Great Invocation

The great invocation was given to a channeller called Alice Bailey by a Tibetan Spirit, called The Tibetan who taught her in the 1940s. She wrote many books on esoteric and spiritual teachings based on the information she received from him. *The Great Invocation* captures the spiritual essence of Reiki. Is it a coincidence that it comes from Tibet?

THE GREAT INVOCATION

From the point of Light
within the Mind of God
Let light stream forth into
the minds of men.
Let Light descend on Earth.

From the point of Love
within the Heart of God
Let love stream forth into
the hearts of men.
May Christ return to Earth.

From the centre where the
Will of God is known
Let purpose guide the little
wills of men
The purpose which the
Masters know and
serve.

From the centre which we
call the race of men
Let the Plan of Love and
Light work out.
And may it seal the door
where evil dwells.

Let Light and Love and
Power restore the Plan
on Earth.

Level II

CHAPTER 11

Level II Reiki

The next step in Reiki following Level I is Level II. It can be taken 21 days after Level I, but it is advisable to wait about three months. This is to allow the practitioner's body time to adjust to channelling energy and to give the practitioner an opportunity to experience the changes brought about by Level I.

The Reiki II workshop is known as the 'wobble' workshop. The reason for this is that the practitioner may experience more indecision about taking Level II than either Level I or Level III. There is a part of him/her which is very keen to take the workshop, but there is also a great fear of doing it. Both these aspects appear to do battle for some time before the practitioner finally makes a decision. The reason for this is possibly that it is a major step forward in empowerment, and brings about great changes. There is a part in all of us which fears change, even if it is for the better. That part of us says do not do the Level II workshop. The part of us that strives towards empowerment, peace and light tells you to do it. Therefore, for many people, Reiki II is only taken after a great amount of soul searching.

FREQUENTLY ASKED QUESTIONS ABOUT LEVEL II REIKI

Q. What will I learn in Level II and how will I benefit by taking this course?
A. There are three main reasons for pursuing Reiki to the second level. The first is that it makes Reiki more user friendly and efficient. After Level II, the channels are at least three times stronger, so you can get much more efficient results on yourself and others. Symbols are also taught at Level II, one of which allows a practitioner to send Reiki to a person who is not physically present. This is known as long-distance healing. This means that Reiki can be sent to somebody who is not in physical proximity to the practitioner, maybe even on the other side of the world, with exactly the same effect as if he/she were in the room with the practitioner. The second reason for choosing to do Level II is that it allows the practitioner to work on situations in his/her life as well as working on physical healing, e.g., his/her business, hobby, relationship, or everyday life. The third reason for taking a Level II course is that it allows more varied use of the energy. It allows the practitioner to release energy from situations that are negative by using the mental/emotional healing symbol, as well as empowering and energising situations and people.

Q. When will I be ready to take Level II
A. As mentioned above, it is best to wait at least 21 days after taking Level I.

Q. What will the workshop consist of?
A. The Level II workshop consists of studying three symbols which have specific uses and effects on the Reiki energy. The first symbol is the long-distance symbol. By using this symbol you are able to treat someone

who is not physically present and it also allows you to influence situations in your past or future. It is what I refer to as 'remote control Reiki'.

The second symbol is known as the mental/emotional healing symbol and is used to alter the energy so that it has a calming effect.

The third symbol is the empowerment symbol. This amplifies the energy, and is known as the 'volume control switch'.

During the Level II workshop you learn these symbols and the various uses of them.

Q. How will a Level II Reiki workshop affect my life?
A. The Reiki II workshop may bring about the following changes in your life:
1. Improved health because the Reiki energy will be much stronger in your body;
2. A much more powerful experience of channelling Reiki;
3. More immediate results from working with Reiki;
4. Increased mental clarity;
5. Greater ability to surrender your life to the energy;
6. Greater efficiency and impact in your working life;
7. A more universal experience of life because you will be more spiritually in tune with life;
8. Greater ease in your life because of using the long-distance symbol to heal any strife in your life before this actually arises, and more likelihood of living from a place of action rather than reaction because you will be more in tune with your conditioning and subconscious patterns.

CHAPTER 12

Symbols and their Uses

THE FIRST SYMBOL
THE LONG-DISTANCE SYMBOL: Hon Sha Za Sho Nen
PRONOUNCED: Hone Shah Zay Show Nen
TRANSLATION: The Buddha in me sees the Buddha in you.

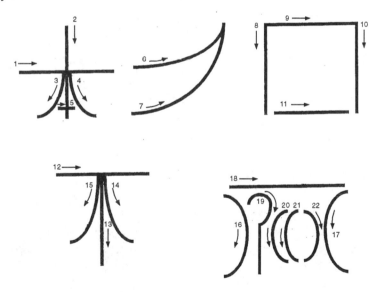

Figure 38

The word 'Buddha' in the translation may be replaced by another if the practitioner feels uncomfortable with it. Common substitutes are: Christ, Spirit and Oneness. The word 'sees' may be replaced by the word 'greets' if this feels more appropriate.

The colour of this symbol is white on a violet or indigo background. The element is air. The long-distance symbol allows the energy of the sender and the receiver to become one. This symbol is used to:

1. Open and close all sessions;
2. Send healing to a person's past (including past lives) and future life to the time of their death or beyond it;
3. Heal any situation in a person's life;
4. Heal any negative situation before it actually happens by sending it to the day ahead;
5. Train a person in a technique such as horse riding, by sending it energy as opposed to practising it;
6. Develop a business;
7. Perform long-distance healing, when the practitioner and client are not in physical contact with eachother;
8. Heal parts of one's body which cannot be touched;
9. Heal world situations, and
10. Open up the energy or close it off in the first and last positions in a hands-on Reiki treatment as it has a different frequency to the other two symbols.

The practitioner is advised to limit the time of a long-distance session to 20 minutes. This prevents the practitioner or the recipient from becoming over-tired. However, once the practitioner is comfortable with handling the long-distance energy, he/she may wish to lengthen the time of a session.

It is very important that the practitioner remembers to close off with the long-distance symbol. Practitioners find that if they do not close off from the client's or situation's energy, they may become quite tired as the client/situation continues to draw energy through them. I have noticed that not all Reiki Masters teach the practitioners to close off, and this is a very dangerous situation to allow, as the practitioner will remain connected to all his/her clients and will eventually become exhausted.

THE SECOND SYMBOL
THE MENTAL/EMOTIONAL HEALING SYMBOL: Sa He Ki
PRONOUNCED: Say Hay Key
TRANSLATION: I have the key

Figure 39

104

The second symbol is known as the mental/emotional healing symbol or, as Ms Takato called it *the conscious healing symbol*. It is written in Sanskrit as *Sa He Ki*. Ms Takato said of it: *I have the key to the greatest peace.*

This symbol is used early on in a treatment to relax the client so that he/she can get the most benefit from Reiki. The colour associated with it is blue and the element is water. This symbol is best used for about ten minutes in a hands on session and for about four minutes in a long-distance session. However, the practitioner may feel that it would be useful to give more. Up to 20 minutes is acceptable in a hands-on session, and 8 minutes in a long-distance one.

This is the only time that a practitioner must keep his/her mind clear and focused as this symbol provides a direct link to the client's subconscious. The practitioner should concentrate on the symbol, his/her own breathing, his/her grounding, and on any sensory feelings received. This gives a practitioner something to think about that will not interfere with the client's psyche, as it is impossible to keep your mind blank for 10 minutes.

This symbol is good for *depression, anger, sadness, addiction* or any *memory problems*. It *illuminates blockages, clarifies problems and helps to release suppressed emotions and trauma. The mental/emotional healing symbol* also *brings insight to help you resolve problems.*

When using the mental/emotional healing symbol on others, it is normally done with one hand on the forehead and the other cradling the back of the head as shown in *Figure 40*. This position may be held for 10 minutes. It may be used in any of the other positions, if the practitioner feels it is necessary. You will know intuitively where it is needed, or you will see the colour blue in your mind's eye and this will give you an indication when to use the mental/emotional healing symbol. Normally 10 minutes is a sufficient amount of time in a hands-on session for using *Sa He Ki*.

This symbol can also be used after the empowerment symbol in order to change the effect of the energy. It is particularly useful on the abdominal area, as often the client will find it difficult to receive Reiki in this area of his/her body. The empowerment symbol is used to activate the energy and when it is felt it can be changed to the mental/emotional healing symbol so that the effect on the client will be very gentle when releasing any blocked emotions from this area.

Once again some masters teach their students that the empowerment symbol should be used prior to the mental/emotional healing symbol but either may be used independently or together.

HAND POSITIONS FOR THE MENTAL/EMOTIONAL HEALING SYMBOL

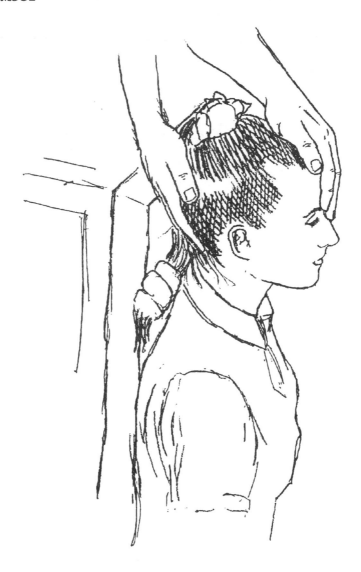

Figure 40

THE THIRD SYMBOL
THE EMPOWERMENT SYMBOL: Choku Rei.
PRONOUNCED: Cho Koo Ray.
TRANSLATION: I command the Universal Energy.

Out-version

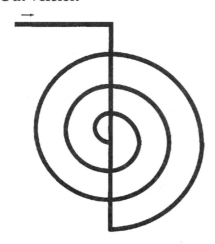

In-version

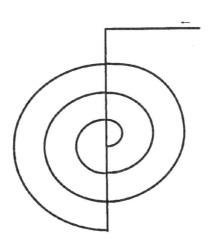

Figure 41

This is the third and final symbol taught in Level II. The colour associated with it is red and the element is fire. The purpose of the empowerment symbol is as follows:

1. To *activate* the *energy* in an efficient manner, as opposed to waiting for the energy to come through at its own rate as in Level I;
2. It acts as a *volume control* by amplifying the intensity of the Reiki energy;
3. It acts as a *protector* by sealing out unwanted energy, e.g., in a room, car or food;
4. It helps to activate *other symbols*, and
5. To *clear a space* of any negative energy: the practitioner stands at the centre of the room and makes the outgoing symbol in each of the four directions.

There are two ways of making this symbol. When it is used in an *anti-clockwise* direction it sends energy *outwards*, and in a *clockwise* direction, it brings energy *into yourself*. Usually the 'in' form of this symbol is used as a blessing for yourself. The 'out' version works as well as the 'in' version on the individual body parts of the practitioner. To bless yourself using the 'in' version, simply bring your right hand across the chest to the heart, moving vertically down the middle of the heart and making three progressively smaller circles in a clockwise direction over the heart. Finish by touching the heart physically with your hand.

Finally, many practitioners find the empowerment symbol useful in clearing traffic jams, and in assisting themselves to get from place to place quickly. It has even been known to change traffic lights. Many practitioners speak of their car working in such a manner as to keep the practitioner safe. The practitioner finds that if there is danger ahead of him/her on the roadway, the car will actually lose power in order to allow that danger to pass before the practitioner arrives on the spot. So, if following a Reiki course your car acts erratically, do not dispose of it: it is not the car, it is the Reiki!

SUMMARY OF THE KEY FUNCTIONS OF THE THREE SYMBOLS

The *empowerment symbol* works very powerfully on the physical body. The *mental/emotional* healing symbol works powerfully on the *mental* and *emotional* body and the *long-distance* symbol works by *opening* and *closing* the energy. However, Reiki energy cannot easily be boxed in and there is a certain amount of overlap of the symbols. Should the practitioner use an incorrect symbol, Reiki will ignore it and send the correct frequency.

HOW TO GIVE A HANDS-ON TREATMENT USING THE REIKI SYMBOLS

A.
1. The practitioner decides if he/she will start with the client either lying face down or face up.
2. When starting with the client lying *face down* make the long-distance symbol and place the hands as in *Figure 14*. Hold this position for four minutes.
3. Go through the remaining positions on the back using the empowerment symbol, holding each for four minutes.
4. When the client is lying face up, commence with the hands under the head (see *Figure 1*). Use the empowerment symbol in this position for four minutes.
5. Leave one hand under the head, and place the other hand on the front of the head, and use the mental/emotional healing symbol for 10 minutes (*Figure 40*).
6. The next three positions (see *Figures 2, 3* and *4*) can now be omitted.
7. Move to the throat/neck area (see *Figure 5*) and use

the empowerment symbol for four minutes
8. Move down the body using the empowerment symbol in each hand position for four minutes. Sometimes an extra 10 minutes of the mental/emotional healing symbol is used. The practitioner will be guided to use it, either by an inner sense of knowing, seeing the colour blue or water, or hearing *Sa He Ki* inside his/her head. The most common areas to use it further are the heart and abdominal area.
9. When the practitioner reaches the last hand position (*Figure 13*) he/she uses the long-distance symbol for four minutes. This indicates to the energy that the session is almost over, and to finish any final work.

B.
Should the practitioner commence with the client lying *face upwards,* the sequence is as follows:

1. Begin by making the long-distance symbol and placing the hands under the head (*Figure 1*) for four minutes.
2. Leave one hand under the head and place the other hand on the front of the head. Make the mental/emotional healing symbol and hold for 10 minutes as in *Figure 40*.
3. Move to the throat area and use the empowerment symbol for four minutes. Continue with the empowerment symbol on each area, unless guided to use the mental/emotional healing symbol.
4. When the final position (*Figure 20*) is reached use the long-distance symbol to close off.

LONG-DISTANCE HEALING

A.

To send long-distance healing, the following procedure is followed:

1. Make the long-distance symbol.
2. Tell the energy what it is to do. I always imagine that I am speaking to the Genie from Aladdin's lamp.
3. Make the empowerment symbol three times, saying it three times in Sanskrit and three times in one's own language.
4. The practitioner holds his/her hands with the fingers extended, hands facing towards eachother, about 25cm apart.
5. It is important that the practitioner's elbows are not resting on anything, as the energy will move the practitioner's hands and arms around.
6. Should the practitioner feel that the mental/emotional healing symbol is needed it can be added at any time for up to 6 minutes.
7. Once 20 minutes have elapsed the practitioner may then make the long-distance symbol to close off the session.

GENERAL POINTS ON LONG-DISTANCE HEALING

1. When possible request the permission of the client to whom you are sending Reiki.

2. When someone is on medication always get permission before sending long-distance Reiki.

3. In general limit the time to 20 minutes. A further 20 minutes may be sent a few hours later.

4. Once six months has elapsed following the practitioner's Level II Reiki course, he/she may use his/her intuition for knowing the correct length of time of a session.

5. The symptoms may become more pronounced during the first three sessions.

6. Long-distance Reiki is much more tiring on the practitioner than hands-on Reiki.

7. There is no need to visualise the client or situation when giving long-distance Reiki. You can treat people you have never met with equal effectiveness as those you can visualise easily.

8. When treating a particular body part, send the energy to the person's entire body, not just the affected area. This is because the cause and affect may be in two different areas.

9. The more situations in life the practitioner uses Reiki for, the less complication will arise in his/her life.

FIVE WAYS OF APPLYING THE SYMBOLS

1. Standing over the client, with the client's eyes closed and making them over the client's whole body.

2. Sitting beside the client and making them over the areas of the body which are being treated.

3. Making them with one's head and projecting them onto the body part which is being treated.

4. The practitioner making them on his/her hands before placing them on the client's body.

5. The power of intention only – the chosen method for elderly people, children and people with learning disabilities.

WAYS OF MAXIMISING THE POWER OF THE REIKI ENER-
GY DURING A REIKI TREATMENT
1. Repeating the symbol each minute during each hand
position.
2. Placing a picture of a spiritual person or deity in the
room and using eye contact with him/her during the
Reiki session. This draws in not only the power of the
Reiki energy but also the spiritual energy associated
with the spiritual teacher.
3. Prayer.
4. Repeating the name of a spiritual person or deity
while channelling Reiki.
5. Use the mental/emotional healing symbol very early
on in the treatment.
6. The practitioner keeps him/her self very relaxed by
concentrating on his/her breathing, grounding, keeping
his/her eyes closed and allowing his/her body to
become a river of energy.

CHAPTER 13

Most Commonly Asked Questions During a Level II Workshop

Q. When I am doing long-distance healing do I require the client's permission?
A. The answer to this question is yes, especially when the client is on some kind of medication, so that he/she will not adjust the medication during the first four treatments. When the client knows that the energy is being sent and at exactly what time, he/she can lie down and relax so that he/she is more receptive to receiving it. Long-distance energy is drawn in by the client in the same way as hands-on energy. The more relaxed the client is at the time, the more receptive he/she will be to the energy.

However, if the client is not taking medication and if the practitioner is unable to contact him/her for any reason, simply ask the client's higher self or the client's subconscious for permission to proceed. The practitioner will receive in his/her mind a clear yes or no. When there is a 'yes' the energy may be sent, and in a situation where there is a 'no' the energy should not be sent. When in doubt, the practitioner may send the energy and if energy is felt to be drawn from the practitioner then it indicates that the client is receiving it. When the practitioner does not feel the energy being drawn from him/her, it indicates that the client is not receiving the energy and the practitioner may discontinue channelling.

Q. Why should the practitioner limit long-distance Reiki to 20 minutes?
A. Long-distance Reiki is three times more powerful than hands-on Reiki. Both giving and receiving Reiki creates certain changes which the body needs time to integrate. For this reason, it is best to stop after 20 minutes, but it is perfectly appropriate to send a further 20 minutes worth of the energy a few hours later, if the practitioner feels it is needed.

Q. How does long-distance Reiki work?
A. Reiki has the ability to set aside both time and distance. Therefore Reiki will work on any situation in the past or in the future. A possible explanation for this is that everything happens on the energy level. Reiki works on changing the energy so the experience is changed. Exactly how the energy travels from the practitioner to the client/situation is as yet unknown. It may happen in much the same way that a telephone can be used if connected by wires or without wires, i.e., mobile telephones.

I can vouch that long-distance Reiki works just as well as ordinary Reiki. When my cousin had a collapsed lung as a result of pneumonia, I worked on him long-distance. The lung was re-inflated in hospital and, although it was not sitting in the correct position, he was sent home temporarily, and was to return one week later for corrective surgery. On receiving his third long-distance treatment, the lung relocated itself, much to the amazement of the medical staff. This was also corroborated by X-rays and an exercise test.

Q. How important is it that the symbols are used correctly both in the way that they are made and the way that they are applied?
A. The symbols should be used exactly as they were taught for at least the first six months. These symbols, however, develop the practitioner's intuitive ability and after six months the practitioner should trust this ability more than the formal teaching he/she received during the Level II workshop. For example, pupils are taught to use the mental/emotional healing symbol for at least ten minutes, but if it comes into the practitioner's mind very strongly to prolong the time, it is probably an indication that the practitioner should continue.

The symbols work by what is known as the power of intention so if, after using them for some time, the practitioner reviews them and discovers that he/she is not using them exactly the way they were taught, the energy will still have worked the way the practitioner had intended. People with learning disabilities do not have to use the symbols, but can simply use the power of intention. The ability to do this comes from the second level workshop and the attunement in that workshop.

Q. Why do I keep seeing a particular shape when I am channelling Reiki?
A. The good news is that this is probably a symbol that is meant especially for the practitioner. There is an infinite number of symbols on an energy level. Dr Usui was given just four of these symbols on Mount Kuri-Yama. Following Level II Reiki it is not unusual for a practitioner to receive a symbol directly from the Spirit, which is intended for his/her own particular use.

Q. *Why do I see different colours when I channel Reiki?*
A. Many practitioners see colours when they are channelling Reiki. Reiki energy stimulates the third eye and non-physical frequencies are seen. Some practitioners see specific colours which tell them that the Reiki is having the desired effect. Other practitioners see walls of colour which have no particular meaning for them. The colours are seen when the brain waves enter a particular frequency. Others see the whole of the client's body as if it were transparent. Some are shown the event which created the present condition in a client's life. Of course you see images in your mind's eye all the time, and after Level II many of these images contain pertinent information for either the client or the practitioner and the practitioner should recognise these as such.

Finally, many practitioners see non-physical bodies, i.e., spirits of deceased relatives of the client, spiritual teachers or guides. This may or may not happen to you, as they are all different forms of clairvoyance. Clairvoyance can be a useful tool in Reiki but it is important to stress that it is not an integral part of Reiki. The practitioner who has strong clairvoyance ability is not necessarily better at channelling Reiki than a practitioner who is not clairvoyant.

Q. *Is it necessary to use all the symbols on a client, even if I am treating only one area of the body?*
A. It is advisable to use all the symbols on a client even if the practitioner has chosen to work on only one area. While the injury may appear on the physical level only, the cause may be on the mental/emotional level. It is always best, therefore, to use all the symbols.

119

Q. When I am working on myself do I have to open and close the energy?
A. A practitioner does not have to open and close the energy on him/her self when doing hands-on Reiki. The practitioner may use the empowerment symbol or the mental/emotional healing symbol as he/she feels appropriate. The practitioner must however, use the long-distance symbol when working on the parts of his/her body which he/she cannot reach.

Q. Do I always have to open and close the energy using the long-distance symbol?
A. No, not always. When working on yourself, you may simply use either the mental/emotional healing symbol or the empowerment symbol.

The empowerment symbol may be used independently as a sealer or protector.

Q. What happens if I forget to close off the energy?
A. This means that the practitioner's and the client's energy remain connected. This leads to a continual draw through the practitioner resulting in emotional and physical depletion in the practitioner.

My Reiki Master had an unpleasant experience with this problem. Before going to sleep he decided to send energy to his father who had severe bronchitis. He fell asleep while sending it and woke up at 4 a.m. and found he had difficulty breathing. He remembered that he was still connected to his father, closed off the energy and was able to breathe normally once again. This illustrates the importance of closing off.

Q. What if I am unsure if I closed off or not?
A. When the practitioner is unsure whether he/she has closed off, he/she may make a long-distance symbol to close off from anything which he/she is attached to.

LEVEL III

CHAPTER 14

Questions Most Frequently Asked by Practitioners About the Master's Workshop

Q. Why should I take a Master's workshop in Reiki?
A. The Master's course may be taken for any or all of the following reasons:
a. To enable the practitioner to have a greater impact in his/her life.
b. To have a stronger connection with other life forms on the planet, both physical and non-physical.
c. To strengthen the life force within him/her self.
d. To have increased healing ability.
e. To initiate other people in Reiki.

Q. What criteria are necessary to take the Master's Reiki course?
A. One should have taken Level I Reiki at *least one year* prior to taking the Master's course and one should have taken Level II Reiki at least *six months* prior to it. One should also *have practised Reiki* on a regular basis prior to taking the Master's Level. The practitioner requesting to do the Master's Level must also be in *good physical* and *emotional health*. The last criteria is that the practitioner should *feel a desire* to do the Master's Level in Reiki at this particular time, as in many ways it is the Reiki

energy that chooses the practitioner to become a Reiki Master.

Q. What changes will take place in my life as a result of taking my Master's Level in Reiki?
A. The changes are very similar to those which took place after Level I and Level II Reiki, except that they are more pronounced. Any weakness in the body could temporarily be exaggerated when healing is activated on a very deep level. This could be accompanied by emotional changes when trapped emotions are released from the body. The first few months following a Master's training course can feel like an emotional roller-coaster: incredibly wonderful at times and very confusing at other times. There is more of a need to have quiet times to allow emotions to come to the surface and heal.

Spiritually, of course, there is a much stronger connection with the Reiki energy, both during Reiki sessions and in general life. Creation continues to unfold many magical moments, in what one would previously have considered mundane. This results in a greater ability to love life and consequently one attracts love and well-being to yourself.

The Reiki Master develops a very strong connection with his/her spiritual teacher and with the source of the Reiki energy. A Reiki Master has a much greater appreciation of the abundance and the graciousness of the Reiki energy than he/she did following a Level II Reiki course. This results in a feeling of increased safety in his/her body, and develops within the Reiki Master very spiritual qualities such as wisdom, understanding, strength, patience and a desire to share his/her well-being with everyone and everything that he/she encounters. The Reiki Master finds him/her self motivated more from his/her heart than from a need for ego gratification or from greed. Such destructive qualities are replaced by love.

Career wise, one might also make some changes. It is not unusual for Reiki Masters to start another career after taking their Master's in Reiki, or to set up their own business.

Relationships can be a little difficult in the sense that one feels the need for integrity in all aspects of personal and professional relationships. This could be intimidating for the newly qualified Reiki Master's friends and associates, and he/she should balance this integrity with wisdom, and apply it in a gentle non-threatening manner.

Q. Who is it best to take my Reiki Master's Course with?
A. The best Master to study with, as in Level I and Level II, is someone who will be available following the workshop to give any assistance that is required. One should feel comfortable with one's Master as there will be a life-long connection with him/her. Quite often issues arise between Reiki Masters and his/her Master, so there needs to be mutual respect and commitment to resolve these.

Q. Is there any danger in taking a Master's course in Reiki?
A. Provided one is in good health and one has taken Level I Reiki at least one year, and Level II at least six months previously, there is no danger involved. However, if one takes it too soon or when one is feeling weak, either physically or emotionally, the changes may be overwhelming, and can cause either physical or emotional stress.

Q. Why do some Reiki Masters offer the Master's course immediately after Level II?
A. Some Reiki Masters initiate practitioners into Level I, Level II and Level III Reiki without allowing any time interval. Most practitioners are unable to assimilate this amount of change and chaos may arise in their lives. It is a waste of experience and a waste of time as Reiki teaches the practitioner to the degree that he/she is able to receive it. Following each Reiki Level the practitioner's nervous system develops in order to channel the Reiki energy, and it is impossible for a practitioner to move on to the next level of Reiki without this development taking place in his/her body. Also Reiki is learnt directly from the energy and unless one has spent time working with the energy one will not have the ability to incorporate an advanced level of Reiki. A student should always practise Reiki for 21 days after Level I and for three months after Level II and should wait approximately one year after Level I before taking the Master's course. In this way the student will develop the potential to incorporate each attunement and will derive the maximum benefit from each separate level of Reiki.

CHAPTER 15

Reiki Master's Workshop

The following is a programme to use as a framework for the Reiki Master's Workshop. Usually the class is quite small allowing for flexibility, according to the needs of the participants.

DAY 1

- Angel Cards
- Meditation
- History of Reiki

Break.

- Teaching the Master symbol
- Review of Level II symbols

Break.

- Attunements of Level I workshop

Break.

- Review of Level I workshop programme
- Closing meditation
- Home

End of Day 1.

DAY 2
- Animal Cards
- Morning meditation
- Attunement for Level II workshop

Break.
- Review of Level II workshop programme
- Review of the Master's workshop
- Discussion on teaching generally
- Attunement for the master's workshop

Break.
- Review of visualisation and meditation techniques including grounding and centring
- Body work
- Tips for teaching Reiki
- Review of commonly asked questions by Reiki students
- Review of available Reiki material in print.
- Inner Child Cards
- Closing meditation
- Certificate presentation

CUE CARDS

Practitioners use cue cards throughout the workshops for the following reasons:

1. To give the participants more insight into the process that is unfolding for them. Working with energy can be confusing, and it can be difficult when the energy is in full flow to know where one is going. Cue cards help to give a focus to the participant and reduce confusion.

2. To give the participants information from a neutral source. Information received from a teacher may appear unfair or inappropriate to a student, whereas participants more readily accept information from cue cards.

3. To introduce the idea of oneness with other spiritual beings (Angel Cards), animals (Medicine Cards), and with our ancestors (Inner Child Cards).

4. To introduce levity to the workshop.

5. To give the teacher insight into each participant's process.

6. To give the teacher insight into a focus for the workshop. For example, I may pick out the Angel Card *clarity* which indicates to me that I ought to be very clear in my teaching; or the Angel Card *spontaneity*, telling me that I can relax and enjoy myself.

ANGEL CARDS

Angel Cards contain just one word that represents a quality such as joy, light, or grace and an image of an angel or angels acting out that quality. No belief in angels is required to use the Angel Cards. If a participant believes in angels, he/she may call on that angel to assist him/her. Otherwise a participant may focus on developing or strengthening that quality of energy.

MEDICINE CARDS

Medicine Cards come from native American spirituality. Each one depicts an animal. The participant may read a message about the lesson associated with that animal from an accompanying book. Medicine Cards can be used to encourage participants to respect all other forms of life. I believe that animals assist us on our journey in life and join us in spirit during transformational processes, such as Reiki workshops.

INNER CHILD CARDS

Inner Child Cards are based on fables and stories that the participant may have heard as a child. They have very beautiful pictures representing different stories, and again there is an accompanying book with a message for each card. The cards are non-threatening because most of the participants associate the stories with fond memories of childhood. They can be used at the end of the workshop as they are very good for giving the participants an idea of the long term changes that will arise as a result of the Reiki workshop.

There are many other cards available but I find these three sets very helpful and acceptable to the participants.

MEDITATION IN REIKI WORKSHOPS

It is suggested that the practitioner begins and ends each workshop with a meditation. The purpose of the meditation is to:

1. Encourage the participants to relax.
2. Mentally focus the participants on the workshop.
3. Heighten awareness of both the physical and energy bodies and the interaction of both.
4. Help the participants to ground the energy.
5. Strengthen the participant's energy lines with the Source.
6. Give the participants the experience of energy flowing through their bodies.
7. Give the participants direct access to the personifications of the healing energy on the planet.
8. Introduce the spiritual teachers directly associated with Reiki.
9. Empower participants to let go of any distractions and concerns that might draw their energy from the course.
10. Encourage surrender to the healing energy of the workshop.
11. Give the participants an opportunity to set a goal or a personal purpose for the workshop.
12. Balances the energy of the group and connects the participants on a heart level.
13. Clear any negative energy from the workshop space and draw in positive healing energy.
14. Re-enforce the Reiki Principles.
15. Acknowledge and thank the energy and the spiritual teachers, and the participants.

OPENING MEDITATION

1. Breathe in deeply through your nose and breathe out through your mouth. Do this at your own pace.

2. Notice as you do so the gentle rising and relaxation in your abdomen just like the ebb and flow of the tide.

3. This is the emotional centre of your body. Welcome yourself home here – say your own name and say: Welcome home.

4. Above your head imagine your own personal sun. Feel the light of this sun shining down onto your head and warming your hair.

5. Allow this light to light up all the cells of your brain. Feel each cell lighting up like the lights of a Christmas tree.

6. Allow the light to come into your ears, eyes, nose and mouth, until you listen with light, see with light, smell with light and speak with light.

7. Feel a flow of light gently moving down into your neck, flowing out of your neck at the back, and your throat at the front.

8. Feel the light flowing onto your shoulders, dissolving any tensions from here. If there is anybody that you feel badly about leaving behind in order to participate in this workshop, or if there is any situation which feels unresolved in your life, imagine yourself removing it from your shoulders, and placing it in the middle of the room. We will take care of it in a few minutes.

9. Feel the light flowing down to your shoulder blades and to your back bone between your shoulder blades.

10. Allow the light to relax all the little muscles here especially those at the back of your heart.

11. Allow the light to flow down the front of your chest and to fill up all the cells of your breast. This is an area, especially in women, that is very vulnerable and may need lots of light.

12. Gradually feel the light moving in from the front and back to fill up your entire lungs. Feel every breath of air that you breathe being charged with light.

13. Allow the light to surround your heart like a blanket. Gradually feel the energy penetrating into your heart muscles allowing them to let go and relax.

14. When your heart is filled with light, allow it to over-flow down your arms and into your hands. When it reaches your hands you may notice a tingling there or a change in temperature.

15. Allow the light to flow from your upper back down into your lower back, relaxing all the little muscles here and energising your kidneys.

16. Feel the light flowing from your chest down into your abdomen allowing this area to open up.

17. Feel the light now move in from the front and the back to fill up the whole of your abdomen. Feel your stomach, pancreas, liver, spleen, intestines and all the spaces in between being filled with light. This is the emotional and physical home of your body. Say your name now once again, and once more say: Welcome home.

18. Now allow the light to drift down into your pelvis. Feel your sexual organs, hips and buttocks filling up with light. This area provides a vital energy to the rest of your body, so feel that it is being recharged very power-fully. Now notice your tail bone and imagine a trap door opening here and a cord of light flowing out of here into the floor beneath your chair, in the shape of a tree trunk.

19. Now allow the light to overflow down both thighs, into both knees, down into your shins and calves. Finally feel it flowing into your ankles and feet, filling up each of your toes.

20. When the light reaches your feet you will notice a tingling sensation, or a change in temperature.

21. Now open up two trap doors, one on the sole of each foot and allow the light to flow into the earth via the energy cords in your feet and also from your tail bone. Allow any unwanted energy from your body to exit via these pathways. The earth will recycle it.

22. Now draw energy up from the earth via these energy cords. The energy from the earth is a nurturing stabilising energy and gives a feeling of security to your physical body.

23. Imagine this energy coming out the top of your head and going up to the heavens to connect with the universal energy source. To help you visualise this, it might be helpful to imagine that you are plugging yourself into the infinite source of energy. As you do this you may notice a particular sound or colour.

24. Now draw the light back down towards you until it reconnects with your own individual light source.

25. Once again notice the light in your heart overflowing down your arms.

26. Join hands with the person on your right and then on your left.

27. Send light from your heart down your right arm to the person on your right.

28. Now feel yourself receiving light from the person on your left.

29. Notice a vortex of light going all around the group, connecting it hand to hand, and heart to heart.

30. Release the hands of the person at either side of you.

31. Continue holding the image of the vortex of light connecting us together so that as well as working as individuals we also work as a group throughout the workshop.

32. Now imagine blowing into this vortex, as if you were blowing up a balloon so that it surrounds the whole room.

33. Blow into it once again until it surrounds the outside of the building.

34. Ground this vortex of light into the earth by imagining it sinking deeply into the earth, and then expand it up into the heavens.

35. Command anything within this vortex that is not in harmony with light and healing to ground itself out into the earth.

36. Call now on the angel you were given on your Angel Card. For those people who do not believe in angels, simply call that quality of energy to yourself.

37. We now call on the spiritual teachers of Reiki to be present – Dr Usui, Dr Hayashi, Ms Takata and Buddha. We call on those teachers of Reiki whose names are unknown, or have been erased from history to be present too.

38. We call on your own spiritual teachers to be present with you over the weekend and especially during the attunement, and to adjust the energy to suit your own particular needs.

39. If there is any person or any situation which you feel could benefit from this workshop, simply place them or the situation somewhere in the space for the weekend and allow the Reiki energy to work on them or on the situation.

40. Finally, in return for investing your time, energy and money here this weekend and working to enhance the spiritual energy of the planet, your family and yourself, ask the infinite energy to give you a gift of something for yourself in return. This could be something physical, for example a new car, the resolution of some unresolved situation in your life, or it could be a quality you wish to develop in yourself. Whatever it is, ask for it now and know that this or something better will come to you.

41. Take a deep breath in through your nose and out

through your mouth.
42. Whenever you are ready open your eyes.

Generally, after completing this meditation, the participants feel relaxed and inspired to work with energy and especially Reiki energy. The energy connection from heart to heart and hand to hand helps to resolve any personality conflicts that may arise during the workshop. The meditation brings out in everyone a sense of co-operation and compassion which lasts during the entire workshop.

The closing meditation is always much shorter. The main purpose of it is to thank the energy, to centre everyone before returning home, to ensure a safe journey and evening. During this meditation it is best to leave longer pauses in its direction because the energy will have built up in the workshop and pauses allow the participants an opportunity to communicate directly with the energy. For the closing meditation possibly play an inspiring song, because at this stage most of the participants are probably very tired of listening to the teacher's voice! Suggested songs might be *Calling all Angels* which is sung by Jane Sibery or Richard Harris' version of *Desiderata*. The song could then be followed with the following meditation:

1. Once again take some deeps breath, and notice the gentle rising and falling of your abdomen with each breath.
2. Notice the flow of energy from your head down to your feet.
3. Notice your grounding.
4. Congratulate yourself now for all your hard work today. First of all acknowledge your emotional body for allowing itself to let go of fear, pain and suffering, for

having been so courageous, empowering and loving. Congratulate your mental body for being so clever and focused, and for allowing you to learn and integrate new concepts and new ideas during the workshop. Acknowledge your physical body for having opened itself up to receiving this wonderful new energy and for allowing itself to be transformed by it.

Finally acknowledge your spiritual body for having adjusted the energy to suit you and for having made your day so profound and peaceful.

5. Now let us acknowledge the energy and the spiritual teachers associated with the energy who worked with us all day long. We thank them and ask them to continue to work with us for the remainder of the evening and night.

6. Take a few more deep breaths.

7. Open your eyes and remember to make your way home more cautiously than usual.

8. God bless you all.

POWER OF THE MASTER'S SYMBOL

Both teaching and learning the Master symbol is a very empowering process. The symbol allows for all the changes that were mentioned under Question 1 to take place (See page 123). It strengthens both the teacher's and the practitioner's energy. Each time I teach the symbol, I feel my connection with the energy becoming stronger, allowing me to receive more of the Reiki energy every moment of my life. Each time the practitioner teaches the symbol they feel a strengthening of the symbol within themselves and a corresponding release of trapped energy. Initially after receiving the Master symbol, the practitioner's experience will be one of love and light. The symbol goes to work on releasing both negative and positive patterns of being in the practitioner in order to facilitate his/her ability to channel the Reiki energy. Unless the practitioner is strong enough to withstand these changes, the body may go into shock in some way, such as developing some kind of lung problem, e.g., asthma.

Once the practitioner has assimilated the effects of the symbol, the rewards are experienced and his/her life is lived from the driver's as opposed to the passenger's seat. He/she experiences the empowerment of the symbol and feels liberated and more in control of his/her life than ever before. The principles of Reiki increasingly enact themselves now through the practitioner, and they are no longer external rules, that need great effort in order to apply them. It is important that the practitioner leaves time after taking the Reiki Master's course before he/she commences teaching Reiki in order to allow time to integrate the effect of the symbol. Teaching Reiki will act as a catalyst for even further transformation, and time is very important to allow for the integration of change following teaching each workshop.

THE MASTER SYMBOL: DI KO MYO
PRONOUNCED: Di Koe Me Oh
TRANSLATED: May the Great Light Shine

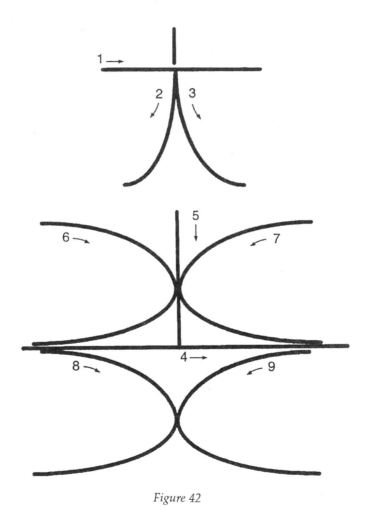

Figure 42

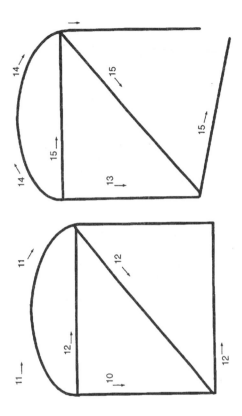

Figure 42 continued

The Master symbol may be used for both *hands-on healing* and *long-distance work* as well as for *transmitting Reiki attunements*. In hands-on work it is especially powerful on the heart but may be used anywhere on the body. It works especially well on the spiritual body of the client and in this way, has a profound effect on the physical, emotional and mental bodies. There is no colour associated with it and no time limit. The master symbol is not used in conjunction with other symbols.

CHAPTER 16

NAMESTÉ

Namasté is a Sanskrit word used as a form of greeting in India and Tibet. Its translation is:

I honour the place in you in which the entire universe dwells.
I honour the place in you which is of love, of truth, of light and of peace.
When you are in that place in you, and I am in that place in me, we are one.

CHAPTER 17

Teaching the Level I Workshop

The following is a programme that can be used for the Level I workshop:

1. *Name*
The participant's reason for taking this workshop.
The participant's history in healing work, if any.
Each participant shares this information with the group in turn.

2. *Angel Cards*
Each participant selects an Angel Card and shares with the group any significance the card may have for him/her.

3. *Meditation*
(As described in Chapter 15)

4. *Ground rules help the workshop to run smoothly.*
Participants agree to:
* Listen when another participant speaks.
* Avoid judgement of another participant's experience or behaviour. (This is to encourage acceptance and respect for each other and to give each of the participants a safe place for expression).
* Express their needs around confidentiality, e.g., if they want material shared to be kept within the group and not discussed elsewhere.

- Drink lots of water during the workshop.
- Walk for 20 minutes during the lunch break.
- Be conscious of his/her grounding during the entire workshop.

5. Review of the workshop programme.
6. The history of Reiki. Definition of Reiki. Discussion on how Reiki differs from other forms of energy and faith healing.
7. *Break.*
8a. Detailed explanation of attunements in general and the first attunement in particular.
8b. Enactment of the first attunement.
8c. Feedback on each participant's experience of the attunement and questions.
9. Teaching of the hand positions on the head and the front of the body including a demonstration.
10. Participants practise the hand positions on the head and front of the body.
11. Sharing experiences of the body work, and discussions of the various sensations experienced. Information given on what you should look for and expect during a hands-on Reiki session.
12. *Lunch break – including a 20 minute walk.*
13a. Explanation of second attunement.
13b. Enactment of the second attunement.
13c. Feedback on each participant's experience of the attunement and any questions.
14a. Hand positions of Reikiing other people when sitting.
14b. Hand positions of Reiki on self.
15. General discussion about Reiki and any further questions answered.
16. Homework.
- Each participant is requested to Reiki him/her

self for 20 minutes that evening.
* Each participant is asked to take not more than two alcoholic drinks and no artificial drugs other than standard medication before returning to the workshop the following day.
18. Closing meditation.
19. Reminder to go home with a little more caution than usual and to avoid any stressful situation until their return for the remainder of the workshop, since they will feel very sensitive as the energy will continue to work with them to release old energy patterns such as grief, anger, etc.

DAY 2

1. Sharing of experiences since the closing of yesterday's workshop.

2a. Explanation of the third attunement.

2b. Enactment of the third attunement.

2c. Sharing of experiences during the third attunement and any questions answered.

3. *Break.*

4. Hand positions on the back of the body.

5. Participants practise body work on the back of the body.

6. Discussion of experiences of the body work.

7. Explanation of the chakra energy system in the body.

8. Demonstration of balancing the chakras in the body.

9. Experiential work with balancing the chakra.

10. *Lunch break – including a 20 minute walk.*

11a. Explanation of the fourth attunement.

11b. Enactment of the fourth attunement.

11c. Sharing of experiences during the fourth attunement and any questions answered.

12. Review of the situations when a Reiki treatment is prohibited

- Lack of a medical diagnosis.
- A psychotic patient.
- A woman in the first three months of pregnancy.
- Lack of knowledge regarding Reiki, what it involves and the possible heightening of symptoms that may be experienced during the first three sessions.

13. Review of guidelines for Reiki treatment (Chapter 8).

14. Review of material available on Reiki and on healing generally.

15. Discussion on looking after yourself (Chapter 9)

16. Inner Child Cards.

17. Effects of Reiki on the practitioner's life following

the workshop (see pages 150 and 151).

18. Presentation of certificates.

19. Closing meditation giving thanks to the participants, the Reiki energy, the Masters of Reiki in spirit, the spiritual teachers of Reiki, and incorporating the Reiki principles.

20. Reminder of monthly follow-up meetings

21. *Home.*

LEVEL I WORKSHOP – FACILITATING ITS FLOW
Eight students is a good number of students for Level I. The core of Level I is four attunements.

These attunements are essential for the participants to graduate in Level I Reiki. The attunements are best given at regular intervals throughout the workshop with the fourth one given at least two hours before the end. The teacher is free to build the workshop around these attunements. It is important for the teacher to address the four levels of Reiki during the workshop. When the channels are opening, toxins will be released from either the spiritual, mental, emotional or physical level or from all of these levels.

THE SPIRITUAL LEVEL
Angel Cards can be used at the beginning of the workshop to support the participants on the spiritual level. Each participant takes an Angel Card at random and then he/she may call on that angel to work with him/her during the workshop. You might begin and end each day with a visualisation/meditation that acknowledges the spiritual teachers directly associated with Reiki – Buddha, Dr Usui, Dr Hayashi, Ms Takato and call upon each participant's own spiritual teachers to be present.

THE EMOTIONAL LEVEL
The emotional level forms a major part of the workshop and it can either create great harmony or disharmony in the workshop. It can create great harmony in the workshop if the participants are properly prepared for it, if everyone in the workshop has an understanding of its source, and if the teacher is prepared and equipped to work with it. The most intense emotions arise during the attunements so it is advisable to try to have some

hands-on body work following the attunements to assist in the integration of these changes, as the direct channelling of the Reiki energy helps the participants to ground and integrate the changes. It is also important never to give an attunement less than two hours before the end of the day, to allow the participant's time to release whatever arises while they are still in a supportive space. Breaks are also essential to give the participants an opportunity to physically move around and to allow time to integrate the emotional changes. It is a good idea for the participants to leave the room during their lunch break. The teacher may then cleanse the room of any negativity by using the empowerment symbol.

THE MENTAL LEVEL

It is very important during a Reiki training to avoid confusion. As various emotional patterns are released by the participants, the participants may project old authority figures or dysfunctional patterns onto the teacher. When the teacher is not clear in his/her teachings it is very easy for the participant to do this. When the teacher is clear that his/her role is to teach and facilitate the participants in learning all aspects of Reiki there is less room for projections or disharmonies between the teacher and participants.

Participants should be encouraged to express their experiences after each section of the workshop and frequent opportunities should be given for questions and answers. It is important for the teacher to realise that science as yet has been unable to explain, measure or quantify Reiki energy and as such Reiki falls into the category of wonder and magic. Many participants who have lived their lives without the experience of wonder and magic will need to have some kind of rational

147

explanation of Reiki, as well as the practical experience of it to justify and locate it in his/her life.

PHYSICAL LEVEL

Physical changes will be experienced by each member of the group. Toxins will be released from the body and drinking plenty of water will assist in minimising headaches and muscle fatigue. Various symptoms may be experienced in the body, such as pain or tiredness, and these will be more pronounced on the first day, both in the workshop itself and during the following evening when the participants are in their homes.

Food is very good for grounding and also generates an atmosphere of homeliness and security. It is very helpful to have lots of snacks for the participants to eat during the workshop and the participants should also be encouraged to eat a good lunch. I also find that flowers in the main teaching room and in the rooms where the participants practise their body work also help to relax the participants and to generate a feeling of well-being.

ATTUNEMENTS

The attunements are a very sacred part of the workshop. The experience of being attuned is something that most participants will remember for the rest of their lives, long after they have forgotten many other aspects of the workshop. The first attunement attunes the heart chakra, the second attunes the throat chakra, the third attunes the third eye chakra and the fourth the crown chakra.

I always hold a great sense of reverence for the attunements. It is at this time that I experience Reiki at its most powerful and feel the spiritual teachers associated with Reiki very close to me. The participants are

148

positioned so that it is easy for me to work around them. I explain the physiological process associated with the attunements (see page 24). I demonstrate the attunement on one of the participants, discuss any concerns and review with the group what the possible experiences may be (see pages 23 and 24). I place some frankincense essential oil on my hands. This assists me in the attunements by enhancing my spiritual awareness, and helps to create a sacred atmosphere.

Following the attunements, the teacher could explore with each participant his/her unique experience with that attunement. It is interesting to note that quite often participants experience the energy strongly either before or after the teacher has worked with them, and the participants are asked to stay in a meditative space both before and after their attunement, as the attunement may actually take place prior to or after the teacher has worked with them. It is important to remember always that it is the *Reiki energy* that *attunes* the *participant* and not the Reiki Master. The Reiki Master simply makes it possible for the energy to work by providing a sacred atmosphere and a physical setting for it.

THE ATTUNEMENTS
You will receive these from your Master.

THE FIRST ATTUNEMENT
The most common experience of the first attunement is curiosity mingled with awe.

THE SECOND ATTUNEMENT
Most participants experience the second attunement as physical sensations in the body such as aches, pains and changes of temperature. This is often accompanied by coughing as it works on the throat chakra.

THE THIRD ATTUNEMENT
It is often accompanied by visual pictures such as walls of purple or blue light, kaleidoscope-like images or images of various spiritual teachers or ancestors of the participants who are no longer in their physical body.

THE FOURTH ATTUNEMENT
The fourth attunement is usually a very deep meditative experience.

HAND POSITIONS FOR REIKI
Please see Section 1 of the book.

LOOKING AFTER YOURSELF
Please see Chapter 9 in Section 1 of the book.

THE EFFECT OF REIKI ON THE PRACTITIONER'S LIFE
Level I Reiki will bring about several changes in the practitioner's life following the workshop and these changes should be discussed.

The changes, of course, will be particular as well as general. Using the Inner Child Cards will certainly give some indication to the individual of the changes that are likely to occur following the workshop.

Changes commonly experienced following Level I Reiki are:

1. Heightened awareness of dream states and more colourful and profound dreams. This happens, supposedly, because Reiki helps to make the practitioner's subconscious more accessible. Reiki practitioners also see interesting and varied shapes and designs in their dreams. There is a feeling of being guided and looked after while one is asleep.
2. Out of body travelling to help people who are in need

while they are asleep also occurs. Frequently friends of practitioners report that the practitioner appeared to them in their sleep and worked with them on something that needed healing.

3. There may be some experiences of cardiac arrhythmia. The energy must pass through the practitioner's heart. It will work on healing the practitioner's heart as it does so. The heart needs to become strong and powerful to channel the energy. Various arrhythmias or sudden rapid heartbeats will be experienced by the practitioner to accommodate the energy. The practitioner should be made aware of this as otherwise he/she may feel that there is a physical heart problem.

4. Reiki makes the practitioner cheap drunk, i.e., he/she becomes intoxicated much more easily following a Reiki initiation. The practitioner will now feel quite merry, on for example, two alcoholic drinks where previously it may have taken five or six to achieve the same affect. You also become more temperate and the sensation of drunkenness becomes very unpleasant.

5. There is a tendency towards vegetarianism. Most Reiki practitioners find themselves eating considerably less meat following their Reiki initiation, and many ultimately go on to total vegetarianism. This could possibly be because Reiki gives the practitioner so much more energy that his/her diet can be much lighter, without any discomfort experienced. There may also be a spiritual aspect to this because eating meat involves considerable cruelty to animals.

6. Emotionally, practitioners experience more peace and increased self-esteem following the Reiki initiation. It is very heartwarming to see people coming for their Reiki training who have suffered and worked for years to look after others. Following the Reiki workshop the practitioner spends at least 20 minutes each day loving

him/her self through giving him/her self Reiki. This gives rise to increased self-respect and a willingness to be more assertive on his/her own behalf.

7. There is a release of the reins of life. The energy is like a loving parent, who guides the practitioner through life. Faith in the goodness of life is restored.

CHAPTER 18

Teaching the Level II Reiki Workshop

As stated earlier the Level II Reiki workshop is known as the 'wobble' workshop. Immediately following the Level I Reiki workshop, practitioners become ecstatic about Reiki. The general consensus is that they wish to take Level II at the earliest available opportunity. However, this enthusiasm generally wanes and most practitioners take the Level II Reiki anywhere from six weeks to several years after the Level I. During that time the practitioner may make and change his/her mind several times.

It is important to be aware that the effects of this workshop are experienced prior to the workshop itself. Most participants notice considerable changes occurring in the week *prior* to the workshop. They may experience emotional and/or physical changes. It is very helpful to inform the participants that this will occur, so that they understand what is happening.

The following is a suggested programme for the Level II Reiki workshop. As with Level I, it is a two-day workshop.

LEVEL II REIKI WORKSHOP

DAY 1

1. Welcome
2. The participants state their names and reason or reasons for choosing to take the workshop.
3. Angel Cards.
4. Meditation.
5. Ground rules:
   * Drink water
   * Keep yourself grounded
   * Non-judgemental of other people's experiences
   * Commit yourself to completing the workshop
   * Be patient with the process
6. An explanation of the changes arising in the participants' lives as a result of taking Level II Reiki:
   * Strengthening of the etheric body
   * Mental/emotional healing
   * Empowering the Reiki energy
   * Absentee healing
   * Increasing spiritual integrity
7. Explanation of workshop programme.
8. History of Reiki.
9. Teaching the long-distance symbol.
10. Teaching the mental/emotional healing symbol.
11. Teaching the empowerment symbol.
12. *Break.*
13. Practising long-distance healing.
14. *Lunch break – including a 20 minute walk.*
15. Body work on each other using the three symbols.
16. Closing meditation.
17. Homework.
    - Each participant is requested to Reiki him/her self for 20 minutes using the symbols, and to seal his/her dwelling place using the empowerment symbol.

18. A reminder to the participants to make their way home with a little more caution than usual and to have a very relaxing evening.

DAY 2

1. Participants share relevant experiences since the previous day.
2. Explanation and demonstration of the attunement.
3. The attunement.
4. *Break.*
5. Long-distance work.
6. *Break.*
7. Body work on each other, using all three symbols.
8. General discussion on becoming a professional Reiki practitioner.
9. Medicine Cards.
10. Reiki certificate presentation.
11. Reminder of follow-up support groups.
12. Closing meditation.

TEACHING THE SYMBOLS

The most important aspect of this is that it is fun, otherwise many of the participants may become intimidated. The symbols can be taught on a large board at the front of the room. Each of the participants should be supplied with plenty of paper and black, blue and red pens with which to draw the symbols.

The wording of the symbol should be put at the top of the board in the appropriate colour and the symbol drawn underneath it. Arrows should be provided to give the directions of the lines of energy. The symbols are then intoned, both as a group and individually, to allow the participants to become accustomed to saying them. The participants then come forward individually, and with the left arm outstretched into the air, the symbols are traced with the right hand on the board. By making the symbols on a large scale the participants get a greater appreciation of the impact of each one. This gives them a feeling of empowerment. By having the arm outstretched, the participant receives energy through the arm as well as the top of the head and this will also magnify the impact of the energy.

The teacher could then discuss the functions of the symbol and answer any questions. It is best to start with the long-distance symbol, then teach the mental/emotional symbol and complete with the empowerment symbol, because the most complicated symbol is best taught while the participants' minds are fresh, and the other symbols are then easier to learn. This is also the order that the symbols are used in a hands-on session and in translation this order also makes sense – 'God be with you' (The Buddha in me sees Buddha in you). Then go on to say, 'You have the answer to whatever problem brought you here today' (You have the key), and finally the universal energy is activated to heal the problem ('I command the universal energy').

LONG-DISTANCE WORK

Once the participants have received the building blocks of Reiki it is time to let them build the castle. To do long-distance work, each of the participants chooses a part of his/her body which is in need of energy. The remainder of the participants then send energy to him/her for 10 minutes. Each of the participants is then asked to give feedback in each of the following areas:

A.   Feelings in his/her own body.
B.   Feelings between his/her hands.
C.   Feelings in his/her hands.
D.   How his/her hands may have moved.
E.   Images or pictures that came into his/her mind.
F.   Anything else the practitioner may have picked up.
G.   Finally the person receiving the energy gives feedback to the group on his/her experiences.

This process takes approximately 30 minutes. Given that it is their first time doing long-distance healing, participants find it a very tiring process. For this reason it is advisable to take a break from it after sending it to four people, returning to it at intervals until everyone has practised giving and receiving long-distance healing. There is wonderful amazement and exhilaration on experiencing the energy without any physical connections.

It is advised to always treat a body part rather than a situation, to demonstrate clearly the action of the energy. The teacher may include him/her self in the process as this can be a very spiritual experience for the participants and teacher.

BODY WORK

The participants divide into couples and on Day One, one person gives the other a complete hands-on Reiki session incorporating the symbols. On the second day of the workshop the giver becomes the recipient and the recipient of Day One gives the Reiki session. This is a relaxing and empowering experience both for the recipient and the giver.

SECOND LEVEL ATTUNEMENT

You will receive this from your Master.

GENERAL POINTS TO BE REMEMBERED WHEN TEACHING
LEVEL II

1. Many participants will find the symbols intimidating and may become confused. *Repeat* them at least *seven times* during the workshop so that they are at least in the participant's subconscious before he/she leaves. Remind them that the symbols and the information associated with them are in his/her notes, and that they may contact the teacher at the monthly follow-up meetings after the workshop to clarify anything that remains confusing, or any new issues that may arise.

2. Participants should commit themselves to *completing the entire workshop.* There may be some strong physical or emotional reactions during the workshop, when toxins are released and it is important that the participants complete the workshop otherwise the effects of these toxins may remain with them for some time afterwards. By remaining in the workshop these toxins, or emotional states are resolved in a few hours.

3. *Eight new participants* is a good number for this workshop and it is also helpful when there are two or three participants repeating it. The presence of participants taking the workshop for a second time helps to stabilise its energy.

4. *When the participants are practising the long-distance work on the teacher, he/she should ensure that he/she has a break in the workshop after he/she receives it.* Receiving energy from the participants may give rise to certain reactions on the part of the teacher and these reactions could destabilise the workshop. A lunch break could be arranged following the long-distance energy work as it gives the teacher one-and-a-half hours to integrate the changes.

5. *The Reiki symbols used to be secret,* but this is no longer the case since they have been published in several books

over the past few years. However, participants should be taught to respect these symbols and to use them in a dignified manner. *In public the participants of the workshop are asked to use the symbols in a private fashion, either by the power of intention or using them in a more subtle fashion.*
6. *Hands-on body work is very important in the afternoon of the workshop* as the participants are usually quite tired. The body work helps to integrate the information received and gives the participants a chance to rest.
7. Many emotions can arise for the participants and many unresolved issues may be expressed. *It is important for the teacher not to expect a resolution of all the participants' issues.* Bringing the issues to the surface is very healing in itself, and giving someone Level II Reiki provides the participants with more power to resolve their own issues.
8. *Humour should be encouraged during the workshop,* as in all aspects of life. The lighter the tone of the workshop, the more pleasant the experience will be for the teacher and for the participants.
9. There is a certain magic about doing long-distance work. That magic is there in our lives today as a result of the hard work done by our ancestors. It is very important that the Source of this incredible tool of empowerment is acknowledged during this workshop, and especially the spiritual lineage that makes Reiki available to all of us today. As stated earlier, Reiki can be traced to Buddha, but it is unclear if it existed prior to his incarnation. It was certainly passed along the line by Dr Usui, Dr Hayashi and Ms Takata. There are obviously some missing links which may include the Source itself or it may be other unknown spiritual presences. During the workshops we thank both the named teachers of Reiki, the Infinite Source of Reiki, and the unknown channels of Reiki. It is important also that the participants

161

acknowledge their own passage through time before their present incarnation, which allows for them to have such an incredible transformation of being in such a short time. It would appear that the ground work for the mushrooming of Reiki on the planet is a result of the spiritual development of mankind, with the graciousness and assistance of many spiritual teachers. At this time we can only practise our final principle and say a very big thank you to all concerned.

CHAPTER 19

Prayer to St Francis

The prayer of St Francis encourages individuals to become channels of Divine Grace. It gives expression to the silent action of Reiki.

Lord, make me a channel of Your peace;
where there is hatred, let me sow love; where there is injury,
pardon;
where there is doubt, faith; where there is darkness, light;
where there is despair, hope; and where there is sadness, joy.
Divine Master, grant that I may not so much seek
to be consoled as to console, to be understood as to
understand,
to be loved as to love.
For it is in giving that we receive, it is in pardoning that we
are pardoned,
and in dying that we are born to eternal life.

CHAPTER 20

Teaching the Master's Workshop

MASTER'S LEVEL ATTUNEMENT
You will receive this from your Master.

REVIEWING THE SYMBOLS
It is very important that all the participants in the Reiki Master's workshop are comfortable with all four symbols. These should be reviewed and discussed early on in the Reiki Master's workshop.

TEACHING THE ATTUNEMENTS
The attunements are best practised on a teddy bear or doll before the participants start practising on each other because the attunements release a considerable flow of energy on the receiver, and it is better if this is not done more often than is necessary. Once the teacher is happy that the participants are confident in the attunement process, they may progress from the teddy bear and practise on each other once or twice. They should be reminded that it is the Reiki energy that actually does the attuning and if the attunement is performed in an incorrect fashion, that it still works. The participants should also be reminded to keep the attunement instructions with them during the workshops, so that if they are in any doubt they may check their instructions.

TEACHING SKILLS FOR REIKI WORKSHOPS:

1. *Everything should be explained in advance* to the participants. There should be no element of surprise in the workshops – surprises may be experienced as shocks by the participants.

2. *Avoid excessive personal interactions* with the participants in order to minimise any personality problems or projections. During the workshop various issues of an emotive nature may arise for the participants. Where there is personal interaction between the participants and the teacher in excess of what is required in order to facilitate the workshop, the teacher could become involved in these issues in a negative way. When the teacher stands clearly as the instructor and facilitator of the workshops, and acts in a neutral fashion, it is much more difficult to involve the teacher in such negativity.

3. Apart from the attunements the remainder of the workshops are optional, and while participation should be encouraged, it is not obligatory. When the *participants are given the option of participating or not*, it removes one possible stress situation from the workshops. Participants generally find the workshops quite intense, so it is best to try to ensure that the intensity is at a level which the participants find manageable.

4. It is a good idea to *allow the energy to pair people together* for the body work, but if a couple arrives together and are happy working together they should be allowed to do so. The practitioner could place everyone's name on a card and then the cards shuffled and picked two at a time, and these two people work together. Again this helps to keep the teacher in a neutral position.

5. It is important to *respect time agreements*, and this should be clarified in advance of the workshops. When participants choose to arrive after the deadline, they are then aware that they have missed some of the workshop

and it is their own choice to do so. When the teacher waits for participants who are late arriving for the workshop, or resuming after breaks, the workshop becomes quite disjointed.

6. The participants must be given tools for dealing with anything uncomfortable which may arise during the workshop.

Physical discomfort is minimised by:
- Drinking water
- Keeping him/her self grounded
- Changing the pace of the workshop and including body work
- Frequent breaks
- Providing adequate food

Emotional discomfort is minimised by
- Giving frequent breaks to allow for unwinding
- Keeping the days as short as possible to prevent over-tiredness
- Discussion

Mental discomfort is dealt with by:
- Checking in after each section of the workshop to explore the participants' experience. Using cue cards, such as Angel Cards, also helps to bring awareness to the process

Spiritual discomfort is minimised by:
- Using the participants own spiritual teachers as well as the spiritual teachers of Reiki and the Reiki energy
- Using frankinscence essential oil to raise the spiritual energy
- Playing spiritual music during the attunements

7. *All participants must be treated equally*, for example, instead of asking for feedback generally at the end of each section, ask each participant in turn.

8. Become conscious of any controlling patterns demonstrated by the participants which may interfere with the workshop and take responsibility for these. For example, if one participant repeatedly interrupts the other participants when they speak, he/she should be gently reminded of the ground rules.

9. *Keep your heart chakra open* when addressing each participant sending healing energy from your heart.

10. Really *listen when each participant speaks* and encourage other participants to listen. There is great healing energy in being heard.

11. Do not reply to questions immediately. Always pause, tune into it and *allow the energy to speak through you.* There are no pat answers in Reiki and each answer should be specific to the participant and each situation.

12. *There are no absolutes in Reiki.* A certain number of absolutes are taught in the workshops to act as a foundation for the Reiki in the participants, but the participants should be informed that as they practise Reiki, they should listen to the Reiki itself and be guided by it.

13. *The Reiki principles* and *way of life* encouraged by the principles are as important as the hands-on Reiki work. The principles should be repeated many times in each workshop.

14. *Give each Reiki workshop four advance sessions of long-distance healing,* to ensure the correct blend of participants and to heal anything that might cause discomfort during the workshop.

15. Always *teach the history of Reiki in every workshop* and acknowledge its lineage.

TEACHING MEDITATION/VISUALISATION TECHNIQUES

Meditation/visualisation techniques that are commonly used appear on pages 130-135. It is recommended that participants of the Level III workshop make a tape of themselves guiding a meditation/visualisation before doing so in a class. This will give them excellent feedback about the pacing, tone and pitch of their voice. One of the most important aspects of meditation/visualisation work is timing. Pauses must be left after each section to allow the process to occur but, if the pauses are too long, the participant's mind will drift off and the effects will not be so noticeable. It is helpful to explore the purposes of using meditation/visualisation (see page 130).

It is a good idea for the participants to listen to other meditations/visualisations to get an overall sense of the many different forms and ways of using this technique.

QUESTIONS THAT ARE COMMONLY ASKED DURING A
MASTER'S WORKSHOP

*Q. How do you deal with a client that you feel has been
sexually abused when the client appears unaware of
this abuse?*
A. The first thing that needs to be said about sexual
abuse is that the practitioner should never tell the client
that he/she suspects that the client has been abused.
The reason for this is twofold. First of all the practitioner may be mistaken. Secondly when the client's con-
sciousness is ready to become aware of this information
it will be revealed to the client. In the meantime, the
practitioner treats the symptoms that the client presents.

The practitioner should educate him/her self about
abuse perhaps by reading or taking a course from a
qualified person. Someone abused during his/her childhood may remember the abuse during the first half of a
Reiki session. They may then move into a feeling of
peace and light, gradually becoming more at peace with
themselves by the end of the session. Most clients who
have been abused prefer that the practitioner works
only above the waist, as any kind of touch below waist
level feels invasive.

*Q. Why does the energy sometimes descend upon me like
a cloud and give the feeling of dissolving my body
away?*
A. The experience of channelling Reiki can become quite
intense. During certain treatments, the energy, rather
than confining itself to specific energy channels in the
body, will be channelled through the person's entire
body and auric field. This will give rise to a loss of
awareness of the practitioner's physical boundaries, and
the practitioner will simply feel him/her self as a river
of energy. Typically, this happens when a practitioner

169

has been channelling energy for a few years and the recipient is very receptive to the energy.

Q. What is the best way to use the intuitive ability that arises as a spin-off of channelling Reiki?
A. The best way to use the intuitive ability that arises as a side-effect of channelling Reiki, is to use it for bringing greater healing into your own life and the lives of those people around you. It is best not to use it for personal glorification or as a performance act at gatherings, as this leads you away from the healing pathway.

Q. When is it best to start giving workshops following the Reiki Master's course?
A. It is best to wait six months following completion of the Reiki Master's course before giving workshops. This allows for the assimilation of any changes resulting from the introduction of the Master's symbol into the psyche. Teaching Reiki will bring about a whole other series of changes, and it is best that too many do not occur at close proximity to each other to allow the Master's body and mind time to integrate them.

Q. Why do I feel as if I am a sponge since doing my Reiki Master's course?
A. The reason for this is that taking the Reiki Master's course makes you very sensitive to the concerns and the needs of others. It is important to set boundaries to what you can accomplish and what is best to leave. When a Reiki Master puts excessive strain on him/her self, he/she will ultimately become ill. It is best to treat the role of Reiki Master like any other job by defining your working hours and free time.

Q. Why do some clients feel an additional pair of hands working on them?
A. Some clients feel a pair of hands in addition to the practitioner's hands which could be either from a spiritual helper or pressure from the energy – it varies.

CHAPTER 21

Most Commonly Asked Questions During Workshops

The following is a list of the most commonly asked questions by participants at Reiki workshops. The answers to all of them are to be found in the previous text. Should there be any concern about answering any of them, it is best to research the answer before doing so.

QUESTIONS
1. What is Reiki?
2. What is the experience of channelling Reiki?
3. Where does Reiki come from?
4. Why do I feel shy about channelling Reiki?
5. How may I treat someone without having a treatment table?
6. How do attunements work?
7. How will the ability to channel Reiki affect my lifestyle?
8. Can Reiki be used with orthodox medicine?
9. Will Reiki be effective if the initial four treatments are not given consecutively?
10. Can Reiki be used on a dying person?
11. When doing long-distance Reiki is it necessary to get the recipient's agreement?
12. Why do I feel uncomfortable giving Reiki?

13. When I am channelling Reiki why do I feel the energy sometimes and not at other times?
14. How does Reiki differ from one teacher to another?
15. How long does it take Reiki to cure various ailments and is it effective on every problem?
16. How old must one be to take a Reiki training?
17. Why did I feel so uncomfortable for 21 days after taking Level I Reiki training?
18. When is the best time to take the next level in Reiki training?
19. Why did such wonderful things happen for the first 21 days after taking Level I Reiki?
20. How many Reiki symbols are there?
21. How many levels of Reiki are there?
22. What do the various colours I see when channelling Reiki mean?
23. When I am channelling Reiki I feel as if I am being enveloped in a cloud of energy sometimes. What am I experiencing?
24. I feel as if I have become a sponge since doing Reiki training. Why is that?
25. Who is the best person to practise Reiki on?
26. Are there any dangers with working with Reiki?
27. When I was receiving a Reiki treatment at one stage I felt an extra pair of hands working on me – whose hands were they?
28. When I practise Reiki on myself during the night, I find it difficult to sleep afterwards – what should I do?
29. When I am channelling Reiki I often see unusual designs and patterns – what is their significance in the Reiki treatment?
30. My hands are hot since I did Reiki training – why is that?

CHAPTER 22

Reiki in the Twenty-First Century

Congratulations on doing either one or all levels of Reiki. It is natural that you might want to explore some sort of community organisation to affiliate to. With the mushrooming of Reiki you will have no difficulty finding many teachers and organisations advertising themselves. You will also see Grecian Reiki, International Reiki, and Karuna I, II and III advertised.

Following the death of Ms Hawayo Takata, Phyllis Furomoto claimed leadership of Reiki. However, Barbara Weber Ray has also claimed that Ms Takata had indicated to her that she would be the world leader of Reiki and founded her organisation, The Radiance Technique Association, in the United States. So as you can see Reiki is coming under many different umbrellas. Phyllis Furomoto is trying to protect Reiki by introducing tighter legal controls and closer monitoring of its growth. There are other groups that say neither Phyllis nor Barbara were ever given ownership of Reiki and if anything it is the society founded by Dr Usui in Japan that has authentic authority.

Personally, I work directly under the Reiki energy itself and look for guidance to the Reiki Principles. I believe in the sacredness of the energy and try to pass this on to all the practitioners that I instruct. I believe that Reiki is abused if the guidelines within this book are not followed and if a teacher is not available to provide follow-up guidance to his/her practitioners.

I also believe that Reiki cannot be controlled by a few people in power and that all practitioners must be given as much information as is available. This is the reason why I wrote this book.

Reiki is the most beautiful gift to the world for relieving suffering and supporting inner peace. What is most important is that you use it on yourself and that you attempt to follow the Principles every day.

With love,
Teresa

Bibliography

BOOKS SPECIFICALLY ABOUT REIKI

Arjava Petter, Frank, *Reiki Fire*, Lotus Light, Shangri-La, 1997

Baginski, Bodd and Sharamon, Shalilia, *Reiki Universal Life Energy*, Life Rhythm, 1985

Brown, Fran, *Living Reiki – Takata's Teaching*, Life Rhythm, 1992

Haberley, Helen, *Hayayo Takata's Story*, Archedicm Publications, 1990

Horan, Paula, *Empowerment Through Reiki*, Lotus Light, 1989

Milner, Kathleen, *Reiki and Other Rays of Touch Healing*, K. Milner, 1989

Stein, Diane, *Essential Reiki (A Complete Guide to an Ancient Art)*, Crossing Press Inc., 1995

BOOKS ABOUT ALTERNATIVE HEALING GENERALLY

Angelo, Jack, *Your Healing Power*, Piatkus, 1994

Balch, James and Phyllis, *Prescription for Nutritional Healing*, Avery publishing Group, 1990

Bass, Ellen and Dais, Laura, *The Courage to Heal*, Harper Collins, 1988

Brennan, Ann, *Hands of Light (A Guide to Healing Through the Human Energy Field)*, Bantam, 1987

Chopra, Deepak, *The Seven Spiritual Laws of Success*, Bantam Press and Rider Press, 1996

Carlson Ph.D, Richard, *Don't Sweat the Small Stuff – and it's all Small Stuff*, Hyperion, 1997

Gawain, Shakti, *Creative Visualisation*, Bantom New Age Books, 1978

Hay, Louise L., *You can Heal Your Life*, Hay House Inc.Y, 1984

Kubler Ross, Elizabeth, *Death – the Final Stage of Growth*, Prentice Hall, 1975

Levine, Stephen, *Healing into Life into Death*, Anchor Books, 1987

Morgan, Marlo, *Mutant Message Down Under*, Thorsons, 1991

Norwood, Robin, *Why me, Why Now, Why This*, Century Press, 1994

Siegel MD, Bernie S., *Love, Medicine and Miracles*, Harper and Row Publishers, 1986

Talbot, Michael, *The Holographic Universe*, Harpep Perennial, 1991

Weil MD, Andrew, *Spontaneous Healing*, Little brown and Co., 1995

MAGAZINES

Caduceus, 38 Russell Terrace, Leamington Spa, Warwickshire, CV31 1HE, England.

Kindred Spirit, Foxhole, Darlington Totnes, Devon TQ9 6EB, England.

Network Ireland, c/o Ruth Marshal, Ballydonahane, Bodyke, Co. Clare, Ireland. Telephone/Fax: +353 (0)61 921 642.

CARDS
Angel Cards
Inner Child Cards
Medicine Cards

Cards and Books available from:
Collins Bookshop, Carey's Lane, Cork, Ireland.
Telephone: +353 (0) 21 275 345
Fax: +353 (0) 21 275 489
(Available by mail order)

Also available from Metaphysical Sections of certain bookshops

REIKI ASSOCIATION IN IRELAND
The Reiki Association,
c/o Pat O'Brien,
East Ferry,
Cobh,
Co. Cork,
Ireland.

IRISH REIKI NEWSLETTERS
Reiki News,
Hamilton Lodge,
Turvey Avenue,
Donabate,
Co. Dublin.

Reiki News – USA
The International Centre for Reiki Training and Vision
        Publications
29209 Northwestern Hwy,
529 Southfield
Mi 48034

..ff.:.

REIKI ALLIANCE – USA
Reiki Alliance,
PO Box 41,
Cataldo,
ID 83710,
USA.

REIKI ASSOCIATION – UK
Reiki Association,
c/o Kate Jones,
Cornbrook,
Bridge House,
Cleehill, Ludlow,
Shropshire SYS 3QQ,
England